Sunset

make it your own : Paint & Color

By Jeanne Huber and the Editors of *Sunset*

Contents

7

50

78

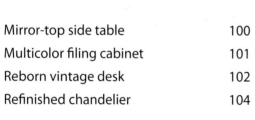

Sunset

©2012 by Time Home Entertainment Inc.
135 West 50th Street, New York, NY 10020

ISBN-10: 0-376-01635-3   ISBN-13: 978-0-376-01635-5
Library of Congress Control Number: 2012932449
First printing 2012. Printed in the United States of America.

OXMOOR HOUSE
VP, PUBLISHING DIRECTOR: Jim Childs
CREATIVE DIRECTOR: Felicity Keane
BRAND MANAGER: Fonda Hitchcock
MANAGING EDITOR: Rebecca Benton

SUNSET PUBLISHING
PRESIDENT: Barb Newton
VP, EDITOR-IN-CHIEF: Kitty Morgan
CREATIVE DIRECTOR: Mia Daminato

CONTRIBUTORS TO THIS BOOK
AUTHOR: Jeanne Huber
MANAGING EDITOR: Karen Macklin
SERIES EDITOR: Anna Nordberg
ART DIRECTOR: Andrew Faulkner
PHOTO EDITOR: Philippine Scali
PRODUCTION MANAGER: Linda M. Bouchard
PROJECT EDITOR: Sarah H. Doss
COPY EDITOR: Barbara Feller-Roth
PHOTO COORDINATOR: Danielle Johnson
TECHNICAL ADVISER: Scott Gibson
SENIOR IMAGING SPECIALIST: Kimberley Navabpour
PROOFREADER: Lesley Bruynesteyn
INDEXER: Marjorie Joy

FRONT COVER PHOTO: The projects in this book inspired this creative display. We painted the room based on the instructions on page 44, and painted the window trim based on the instructions on page 52. Then we updated and refinished the picture frames and buffet table by slightly adapting the instructions on pages 97 and 102.

To order additional publications, call **1-800-765-6400**
For more books to enrich your life, visit **oxmoorhouse.com**
Visit Sunset online at **sunset.com**
For the most comprehensive selection of Sunset books, visit **sunsetbooks.com**

IMPORTANT SAFETY WARNING—PLEASE READ

Introduction

At *Sunset,* we love to reinvent spaces, and color is one of the most powerful ways to do that. It can influence your mood, make rooms feel bigger, and instantly telegraph your personality. Whether you've recently bought a house, moved into a new rental, or plan to spruce up your current home, there are endless ways to add color to your home—and your life.

In this book, you'll find ideas for refreshing any room in your home. You'll learn how to transform an entire space with an expert paint job, create your own innovative wallpaper, sew stylish Roman shades, and paint designs and stencils onto walls, floors, and furniture. We'll also show you how to turn an antiquated dresser into a sleek centerpiece, re-cover a chair with fresh fabric, and add new life to old candlesticks and picture frames. Want to paint stripes on the walls of a kid's room? Repaint your claw-foot tub? Yep, we can show you how to do that, too.

Sure, it might seem easier to call in the contractors or painters, but it'll cost you a bundle—and the process will be a lot less rewarding. There's nothing quite like finishing a project or adding a final paint stroke, then stepping back to see the beauty you've created. And the best part: You get to see your masterpiece every day because it's now a part of your home!

The projects in this book range in the amount of time and expertise they take—and that will vary, too, from person to person depending on where your talents lie (like whether you're better with a hammer or a sewing needle). Start with something within your comfort zone and slowly build your skills until you can take on any project in this book. We know how rewarding it is to design your home to be exactly the way you want it, and we hope this book will help you create a living space you love.

The Editors

1

Find your style

Style isn't just about your favorite colors. It's about the way you want to live. Your style is a reflection of your personality; it's who you are and how you want to project yourself to the world. That's why it's so important to be authentic and genuine when you make decorating decisions. If your style feels right, it will make you happier and more comfortable in your home.

Find Your Style

Here are some examples of traditional styles. Of course, your home can reflect more than one—your bathroom could be Romantic, and your living room could be Natural and Earthy. Feel free to mix and match. Romantic Boho and Playful? Why not!

Clean and Modern
Simple, with clean lines and no clutter—perfect if you like the feeling of being in a spa or a minimalist art gallery.

Romantic
Floral fabrics, warm colors, decorative lighting, and soft-edged furniture.

Boho
Lots of prints, patterns, global touches, and color.

Cozy
Overstuffed furniture, throw rugs, plush pillows, and warm colors.

Natural and Earthy
Organic materials, mellow colors, and wood furniture.

Fun and Playful
Bright colors and bold designs, such as striped or decoupaged walls, and whimsical furnishings.

Quick Tip: Name Your Style
Coming up with an original name for your style, such as Natural Chic or Cozy Boho, is a great way to pinpoint the look you want. And it will help you stay true to your vision when choosing paint, fabric, and wallpaper.

Be a Practical Designer

The best style is also practical. As you create visions for each room in your house, consider the following factors.

How Will You Use the Room?
Be realistic when answering this question! You may think the den will be used for entertaining your book club every Wednesday night. But your husband (or wife) may be banking on it as a place to watch Sunday football games. Consider all the possible uses of the room, and then determine what styles and colors will best suit those functions. For instance, if the space will be used for book club meetings *and* Sunday football, you might want to consider a sectional couch and complementary chairs, which would work well for both. The point is: Style your room based on *all* of the activities that actually take place there—not just one.

What Kind of Light Will the Room Have?
A room's natural lighting will make a big difference in your color choices for the walls, furniture, and carpet. Rooms with a lot of natural light coming in through windows and skylights can handle strong colors, whereas rooms that rely on overhead lighting and floor lamps beg for more subdued colors. You may be dreaming of deep purple for your walls, but if the natural light in the room is low, your room could look more dungeon-like than dreamy. If a room is very small, consider multiple light sources. These can add dimension to a small room, making it appear larger.

What Size Is Your Room?
Does the room feel too big, too small, or just right? Color and design can change the perception of volume. If a room feels too big, use large, soft seating and warm, rich colors to make it feel cozier. For some examples of how to make a small space feel bigger, see page 12.

What's Already There?
You may not have the time or the budget to completely revamp every room in the house. That means you'll probably be working with some existing furnishings, colors, and patterns. As you come up with a vision for each room, take notes about what can go, what needs to stay, and how to best work with all of it. Remember, too, that existing furniture can be revamped and repainted. (See the many projects in this book to learn how to do that!)

Affect Mood with Color

Color is powerful. It's what announces your style in the room. Color can change the visual volume of a space, making it feel bigger or smaller, higher or lower, cozier or more expansive. And it's been scientifically proven to affect people's moods!

Most painted rooms have a primary color, a trim color, and accent colors. Here are the palettes most often associated with the looks described on the opposite page. This is just a guide, so feel free to pick and choose what speaks to you, and add your own preferences and variations.

Cozy
Warm whites, neutrals, pale blues and greens, yellows

Natural and Earthy
Warm whites, beiges, greens, browns

Clean and Modern
Whites, grays, yellows, blues, blacks

Romantic
Light blues, pinks, grays, soft whites

Boho
Vibrant purples, yellows, blues, greens, bright whites

Fun and Playful
Bright yellows, oranges, pinks, blues

Quick Tip: Styling a Kid's Room

Wall stencils and wall decals are easier to add and remove than expensive themed fabric or wallpaper that can't bridge age gaps. Remember, your son or daughter might love rocket ships or unicorns this month, but he or she will probably be over them soon.

Collect Inspiration

So, how to begin finding your style and your colors? You know those pretty style boards that designers put together with photos and color swatches and fabric remnants? Well, you can make one, too. It will help you understand your own preferences for style and color. You can make one style board for your entire house or make one for each room you want to redecorate.

To create a style board, buy a corkboard and some tacks, or do a more basic version with a big piece of cardboard and tape. Fill your style board with magazine pages, photos of rooms that inspire you, colors you love, or vacation photos that evoke a mood you want to re-create. If you have swatches of furniture fabric for the room you're designing or catalog images of things you like, include those too. The more elements you assemble, the more you'll have to choose from in the end. Tack things up and down as you play with the look, and watch your style unfold. And don't despair if your ideas don't seem to blend. This is the stage to go with your gut and experiment!

Once your style board is full, it's time to take stock. Look at everything and see if there are colors or styles that keep showing up. Discard the outliers or anything that doesn't really speak to you. Leave the board up on a wall in your house for a while and see what keeps drawing your eye. Eventually, you'll know which direction you want to go for the various rooms you are designing. Be patient—sometimes it takes a little while before you land on a style you love.

Quick Tips: Alternate Style Board
If creating an actual style board seems like too much effort, you can simply assemble a file or a binder. When you are ready to look at everything together, spread the materials from the file or the pages from the binder on a table or the floor.

Colors and Mood

Style experts say that color can impact your mood. Here are some common color-mood combinations.

ORANGE = INVIGORATING	BLUE = SERENE
YELLOW = WARM	VIOLET = TRANQUIL
RED = ENERGETIC	GREEN = CALM

Of course, everyone reacts differently to colors. Feel free to deviate from the guidelines to match your own preferences and personality, especially in rooms that won't see a lot of company, such as bedrooms and private bathrooms.

A green accent wall in the kitchen may make you feel calmer while you're cooking.

Make a Room Seem Bigger

Small rooms can feel stuffy and claustrophobic, but color and style go miles toward making a cramped room seem bigger. Here are some effective techniques.

Use light colors. Light colors, including white, brighten and reflect light, whereas dark colors absorb light and make a room feel smaller.

Paint one far wall a deep, dark color, such as cobalt blue or a deep gray. This can change the apparent depth of a room. A far wall painted in a dark color tends to extend the gaze, making the space seem to go on forever.

Paint the ceiling the same color as the walls. This creates a cohesive feeling by avoiding a visual line break between the two surfaces.

Use a bold, dark color with lots of glass and mirror accents. Shiny accents reflect light, making the space seem larger even though it's painted with a dark color.

Pair mirrors with a deep purple wall to give a small room an intimate, jewel-box effect.

Paint vertical stripes on a wall. This will trick the eye into thinking the ceiling is higher than it actually is.

Steer clear of dusky or muted shades. These make the room look smaller. Clean colors, no matter what the shade, work best.

Select Your Colors

After creating your style board, you should have a good idea of what colors you like. Bring any clippings or sample color swatches with you to the paint chip wall at the hardware store. Paint chips are free, so collect whatever catches your eye. When you get home, tape these to the wall to see which ones you like best.

Talk to the Pros

When in doubt, talk to the pros at a paint store. Paint store staff can help you select colors and finishes (such as gloss, semi-gloss, and matte). Plus, they can match any color, so feel free to bring in your favorite sweater if you want to see that color on your walls.

Pick the Right White

White is wonderful as an accent or trim color, and as a primary color. When used as an accent, white brings primary colors into sharp relief. When used as a primary color, it provides a crisp, clean backdrop for a room—think art gallery—that lets architecture, furniture, and accessories take the spotlight.

But all whites are not created equal. Whites can be divided into two categories: warm and cool. Warm whites have yellow, red, or brown undertones; cool whites have tints of greens and blues. When choosing whites, be sure to try a few samples in your existing space. Some whites make certain furniture or fabrics look dirty, whereas other whites make colors sing. There is no hard-and-fast rule. Instead, look at the whites in the context of the room to gauge which ones work best.

Create Tints and Shades

You can change colors to make them lighter or darker by adding white or black to the mix. To create a new tint, add white to the paint color; to create a new shade, add black. If the new color is one you'll need to replicate, keep track of the exact amounts of white or black you added to the original color.

Quick Tip: Beware of Glare
If a room is flooded with natural light, very bright white paint will reflect it more and can make the space seem blinding. For naturally bright rooms, choose a white with warm undertones, as pictured here.

Test Your Colors

So you've got your style and color palettes all set. Now it's time to paint, right? Well, not quite. Number one painting mistake: Not testing your colors before painting the room! There is nothing worse than finishing a room, only to realize that the color is just plain wrong. (You might convince yourself that you'll grow to love it, but your gut feeling is right: You won't.)

The solution? Test your paint. Paint chips are famously just a little bit off, so use actual paint, not just paint chips or swatches. Lots of places offer inexpensive sample-size containers so that you can test a few colors on your wall before committing. If you bring paint home and discover that the color you thought you wanted doesn't look quite right, go back to the paint store and see if they can add more pigment or more white to fix it.

Purchase a few sample colors and brush them on the wall or on pieces of paper you can tape up. Let the paint dry, and live with the colors for a few days until you land on a favorite.

Paint is not permanent. That's the reason it's the most favored interior design tool. So go with that bold color palette you've been dreaming about! You can always repaint later if your tastes change.

Add Style with Fabric and Wallpaper

Paint is the most obvious (and economical) way to spruce up a room on your own, but fabric and wallpaper are also ideal for adding color and style. You can change the whole look of a room by simply re-covering the dining room chair cushions (page 94), or wallpapering the panels on your kitchen doors (page 118). These tricks can turn something ordinary into something impressively extraordinary—all without breaking the bank. And you'll never tire of saying, "Oh that? I did it myself."

How to Choose Patterns and Colors

Want to give a room a stronger impact? Pattern and color—in wallpaper or fabric—are an excellent way to do that. Here are a few things to consider.

Vertical elements. Stripes and other strong patterns that go up and down can make ceilings look higher. With fabric and wallpaper, you have a choice of running stripes or stripelike patterns horizontally or vertically, so you can make a wall or a window seem wider or taller depending on how you orient the wallpaper or curtain fabric.

Strong geometric or floral patterns. These can liven up an otherwise lackluster space, but use them sparingly.

Multiple patterns. Avoid using too many different patterns in a room, especially a small room. For instance, if the drapes have a large pattern, avoid wallpaper with another bold pattern or it might compete. Patterns made up of small, repeating elements aren't as risky because they often read simply as texture.

Bold or neutral patterns. This choice often depends on how you use the fabric or wallpaper. If you're tackling a quick accent project, go for something bold and bright. But if you are investing a lot of money and time in upholstery or window coverings, you might want to choose something more adaptable, such as a delicate pattern or an interesting texture.

Bright or neutral colors. Depending on the color you choose, you can make a piece of furniture assume center stage or be more of a supporting piece. For instance, a couch covered in a bright fabric will dominate more than one covered in brown.

Quick Tip: Decisions, Decisions!
Torn between two patterns? Staring at them over and over again can make you even more confused. Instead, simply revisit your style board (page 11) and see which pattern works best with your original aesthetic.

Test Your Wallpaper and Fabric

Wallpaper is often more of a financial investment than paint, so make sure you test the pattern before you buy the whole amount for the project. Many stores and online retailers sell samples that you can place next to your carpet and drapes to see how the colors relate. Of course, you can't preview what a pattern will look like on an entire wall, so consider getting a second opinion from a design-savvy friend. Testing fabric is also a good idea. Even if you're not using very much, see how a sample of the fabric looks in your room against existing furnishings before you invest in a lot of yardage.

Use Wallpaper and Fabric as Accents

You don't have to wallpaper an entire room, or reupholster a whole sofa, to make a statement. Both wallpaper and fabric can be used to smartly accent a room. With wallpaper, you can cover anything from door panels to the hallway stairs; with fabric, you can create a sink skirt, put up a curtain door, or re-cover a few chairs and completely change the look of the room.

Accenting creates an immediate sense of style. A gingham fabric says country, while velvet and lace evoke a soft, romantic look. A retro wallpaper print can take your visitors back to the '50s. Do you like traveling to a certain part of the world? Evoke a sense of India, Africa, or Spain simply by using patterns and colors that are commonly found in those places. The key to creating a striking look is to match your fabric or wallpaper with a few other elements in the room, like candlesticks, a decorative pillow, or picture frames. The best part about accenting: It's inexpensive. You can purchase a small roll of wallpaper or a yard (or less) of fabric, and—voila!—the whole room feels different.

Finally, Be Your Own Unique Self

Designing your home is about designing a place for you to express yourself and feel comfortable and happy. Although it's helpful to research what professional designers and stylists suggest, ultimately your opinion is what counts. Remember: If you love it, it can't be wrong. And, when in doubt, *Sunset* is a fabulous resource. Visit *sunset.com* for endless ideas and inspiration for creating a home you'll love to live in.

Quick Tip: Mixing Patterns
Want to combine a floral print and stripes in one piece
of furniture? Fabric manufacturers often create mixed
patterns that go well together, and they are often
displayed near one another in fabric stores.

2

Getting started

Ready to give your home the colorful make-over it deserves? Before you start painting, cutting pieces of wallpaper, and sewing your heart out, take a few minutes to read this chapter and educate (or re-educate!) yourself on how to prepare for working on your home, what materials to use, and what practices are best. A little background knowledge goes a long way toward making your home projects easier, safer, and more cost-efficient.

Get to Know Paint

Paint is more than color in a can. It's a complex compound that has three main components:
• solvent—the liquid that makes the paint easy to spread
• pigment—the element that provides the color
• resin—the "glue" that enables the paint to adhere to the surface and makes the finish durable

Not all paints are created alike. Here's a cheat sheet.

Latex paint. This water-based paint is often used on walls and ceilings, and is suggested for the majority of projects in this book. It's also referred to as acrylic paint because acrylic is commonly used as the resin. (Ironically, latex paint doesn't contain true latex, which is the milky sap of rubber trees.)

Latex enamel. A specific type of latex paint used for hard-wearing surfaces such as woodwork and cabinets, latex enamel contains more resin than standard latex paint, which makes it dry into a tougher film and stand up to scrubbing better.

Latex porch and floor paint. This water-based paint is made for use on floors. It contains even more resin than latex enamel, and the resin is formulated to be especially hard and scratch-resistant.

Oil paint. This traditional type of paint combines a solvent such as paint thinner and an oil that cures into a hard finish after the solvent evaporates. Oil paint dries harder than latex and is therefore easier to wipe clean later. But we don't suggest it for any projects in this book since it cracks over time, takes longer to dry, and must be cleaned from tools with paint thinner. Some people do prefer it, especially for cabinets and woodwork. If you choose to use oil-based paint for any projects in this book, use an oil-based primer, too.

Spray paint. Available in oil- and water-based formulas, spray paint is ideal for painting items that have intricate details. It contains fast-drying solvents that aren't safe to breathe, so use it only where air circulation is good.

Artist's acrylic. This water-based paint is sold in tubes or small jars, and comes in bright, clear hues. It costs more than other paints, and is usually used sparingly, for artistic effect.

Metallic paint. This water-based specialty paint sparkles like shiny metal. The glint comes from bits of the mineral mica, which are mixed into the paint. (Some metallic finishes do contain bits of actual metal, but their purpose is to tarnish in order to create an antique look.) Liquid gold leaf and liquid silver are similar to metallic paint, but are often oil-based.

Chalkboard paint. A specialty paint that wipes clean when you draw on it with chalk, chalkboard paint is available in the traditional black and green, as well as other colors.

Dry-erase paint. This specialty paint wipes clean when you draw on it with dry-erase markers.

» Latex paint comes in a wide variety of colors and is the best choice for most rooms in the house.

Gloss and semi-gloss paint are the shiniest finishes. They're great for cabinets and trim because they are the easiest to wipe clean.

Satin paint is a little harder to clean than gloss, but works well on cabinets where you want less shine, and walls where you want less shine but will need to clean often.

Eggshell paint is a good all-purpose paint. Its low-luster finish offers a clean, crisp look for most rooms in the house, and it's also washable (though not as much as gloss or satin).

Matte paint looks velvety, so people often use it for places where they want a soft look. But it's hard to wipe clean, so use it in rooms that don't get a lot of wear, like master bedrooms.

Choose a Finish

You've chosen all your colors. You go to the store and hand the paint chips to the person at the paint counter. And then you're asked: What kind of finish do you want? Good question. The name of a finish—such as gloss, semi-gloss, satin, eggshell, or matte—describes the amount of light that the paint reflects. But each finish has other qualities as well. Here are the basics.

Gloss ("glossy") and semi-gloss These paints contain more resin than other paints, which adds shine. The resin also makes the dried paint tougher and slicker, so you can more easily wipe away food spatters or dirty fingerprints.	**Use on:** woodwork, cabinets, and molding with undulating curves and crisp corners.	**Don't use on:** ceilings (because the reflected light highlights surface imperfections and makes the ceiling seem lower).
Satin This paint has less resin and therefore less luster than gloss paint. It's still slick enough for easy cleaning, but the lower shine camouflages surface irregularities better.	**Use on:** cabinets or trim where you don't want a high-gloss look; walls in kitchens and bathrooms that you need to clean frequently.	**Don't use on:** ceilings (for the same reason as gloss paint).
Eggshell Named for the way it mimics the slightly reflective surface of an egg, this paint has a low-luster finish. It's a little more difficult to clean than satin paint, but it hides surface irregularities better. It's a good all-around paint.	**Use on:** walls in rooms other than kitchens and baths where you want a relatively matte look but still need to be able to wipe off dirty fingerprints.	**Don't use on:** kitchen or bathroom walls, especially where the walls might be spattered with oil or soap or need to be scrubbed clean of mildew.
Matte (or flat) This paint has a somewhat rough texture (though you'd need a microscope to see it). The uneven surface causes light waves to bounce back at various angles, resulting in a surface that looks almost velvety.	**Use on:** walls where you want colors to seem especially deep and pure or want surface irregularities to blend in; ceilings; any surface where you've had to do a lot of patching.	**Don't use on:** cabinets, kitchen walls, and any surfaces you have to clean frequently.

However, inexpensive brushes are perfect for touch-ups because they don't hold as much paint so they are easier to rinse clean. Bristle brushes are best for touching up paint that was applied with a brush; foam brushes are good for roller-job touch-ups.

Rollers

To paint a wall or a ceiling quickly and evenly, use a roller. Keep the following in mind while choosing a roller.

Roller cover material. With water-based paint, use a roller cover made of a synthetic material such as nylon or polyester. Mohair and lambswool rollers are for oil-based finishes only.

Nap (or pile) length. This is the thickness of the fabric on the roller head. On smooth walls, use a short-nap roller. On rough surfaces, such as heavily textured walls or fireplace brick, use a longer nap.

Width and diameter. Mini rollers, about the size of a hot dog, are ideal for painting both sides of a corner at once and for applying finish to small areas. Big, wide rollers are most efficient for painting large areas.

Roller frame (or handle). If you are painting ceilings and high walls, consider a roller frame that has screw threads on the end so you can attach an extension handle.

In addition to rollers and brushes, you may also need: ladders; paint trays; razor blades (for cutting tape while masking); a microfiber dust cloth (to remove sawdust); a wallpaper or tile sponge (the best sponge for wiping away residue, because it has small pores that pick up a lot of material); rubber gloves (to protect your skin from harsh cleaning agents); thin disposable gloves (to protect fingers from paint); and nitrile gloves (if you use paint thinner).

Know Your Tools

Some projects are best done with a brush, some with a roller, and some with a combination of the two.

Brushes

A brush delivers paint more precisely than a roller or a sprayer, so it's the best tool when you want to cut in paint at the edges of a room, paint trim, or tackle projects such as painting picture frames (page 97) or the design on the DIY floor mat (page 142). Consider the following options while choosing brushes.

Synthetic or natural. Use a brush with synthetic bristles for water-based paint. Natural bristles swell when damp, making painting messier when you are using water-based paint. Natural bristles are perfect for oil-based finishes, though.

Angled or straight. Angled brushes are ideal for reaching into corners—important if you're painting windows or the cubby-holes in a bookcase (see page 56). Use straight brushes when you are painting wide, flat surfaces.

Quality or cheap. More expensive brushes tend to have more helpful features—such as frayed bristle tips that minimize brush marks. For most painting projects, use these types of brushes.

Quick Tip: Paintbrush Sizes
It's helpful to have brushes in different sizes, such as a small one (1 to 1½ inches wide) for details and a wider one (2 to 3 inches wide) for the main expanse.

Deglossing Shiny Surfaces

If you want to paint over gloss paint or any kind of slick unpainted surface, such as laminate, you need to create a surface that will help the paint adhere. You have three options, and sometimes you may need to use a combination of these.

• Lightly sand with 180-grit sandpaper, just to the point where the surface is evenly dull.

• Put on rubber gloves and wash with a liquid deglosser.

• Use a primer that is made to adhere to slick surfaces that haven't been sanded.

Sanding is quick and doesn't require you to buy other prep products. But liquid deglosser and primer are safer options if you're dealing with lead paint (see page 31). Deglosser is better than primer when you want to preserve crisp architectural details, and you don't need primer for another reason. In many cases, even if you use deglosser, it's good to sand (assuming the paint is lead-free), and this is what we recommend for the paint projects in this book. But if the paint is not chipped, and the deglosser took out all of the shine, you can skip sanding.

« Use an eggshell or matte finish for areas like these, where you want a softer look. If the walls were glossy when you moved in, you'll need to degloss them before painting.

Prepare to Paint

Painting is easy—you just bust out the rollers and get the job done, right? Well, almost. But before you paint anything, you need to prepare for the job.

Clean

If the surface you are going to paint is dirty, you need to wash it. Begin by dusting it with a clean microfiber dust cloth. If the cloth picks up grime, wash the entire surface and allow it to dry before you proceed. Always wash kitchen and bathroom surfaces so you're sure to remove food spatters and soapy splashes. Use water with a few drops of household cleaner, or with liquid deglosser if the surface has a gloss finish. For heavier duty cleaning, you may want to use trisodium phosphate (TSP). It interferes with some primers, though, so check the label first.

Patch

If there are gouges or nail holes in the surface to be painted, fill them before you prime and paint. It's important to use patching material suitable for the surface and the type of hole.

Plug nail holes in drywall. Smear on a little lightweight spackling compound, which has the consistency of whipped cream, with a finger or a putty knife. Try to get the patch material in the holes only. If the holes are small, and if you can avoid smearing spackle on the surrounding surface, you may not need to prime the patches.

Fill dents in drywall. Use a spackle paste here because it has more body than spackling compound. Stir the paste to a creamy consistency. Then use a putty knife to press it into the dents. Apply layers no more than ¼ inch thick, or as the label recommends. Allow each layer to dry before you add the next.

Fill large holes. Use drywall joint compound over fiberglass mesh, which is included in hole-repair kits. Follow the instructions on the package. If the wall has a texture, complete your repair by spraying on a texture material that matches the wall's texture.

Patch holes in wood. Use a water-based wood filler. Slightly overfill the holes, but avoid smearing filler on the surrounding area. When the patches are dry, sand them smooth with 180-grit sandpaper or a sanding sponge.

Quick Tip: Apply Patch in Layers
If you're plugging a deep gouge, apply the patch material in layers. Two thin layers will dry faster than the one thick layer.

Caulk gaps. If you are painting trim, caulk the gaps between the trim and the walls or the ceiling. Use latex caulk that's labeled as paintable. Cut the tip of the caulk tube with a sharp utility knife so it produces a bead the same width as the narrowest gap you want to fill. Recut the tip later for the wider gaps. Apply the caulk in a single pass along each piece of trim, then immediately smooth over it—one time only—with your finger or a dampened rag or sponge.

Sand

If the surface you are painting is rough or the paint is chipped, you can sand it to smooth it (provided it doesn't contain lead—see caution on page 31). If the surface is slick from gloss paint, a light sanding creates little grooves that help the new paint adhere. (If you use deglosser or a primer made for slick surfaces, you may be able to skip sanding; see page 25.) You have two options when sanding.

Sand by hand. This is the best approach on three-dimensional surfaces such as furniture, on delicate surfaces, and on surfaces that need only a light sanding. On a rough surface, begin with a relatively rough grit and work in stages up through finer and finer grits. For scuffing up old paint, use only a fine grit, like 180.

Use an electric sander. When the surface is rough or large, machine sanding can save you time and labor. A palm or random-orbital sander is best for most pre-painting prep; a belt sander is more aggressive, so use it only where the surface is very rough or where you need to remove a tough existing finish. With any type of sander, keep the machine in constant motion. Electric sanders stir up a lot of dust, so wear a disposable respirator dust mask, sold at most hardware stores.

Tape

To keep clean lines, tape adjoining surfaces before you begin. Follow these steps to ensure good results.

Use painter's masking tape. The adhesive on the back isn't as strong as the adhesive on regular masking tape, so when you remove it, it's less likely to pull off the paint underneath or to leave adhesive residue behind. Another option: **Edge-blocking tape.** This is a special kind of painter's masking tape formulated to absorb any paint that seeps under the edge so you wind up with a crisp paint line.

Apply tape carefully. Working in short sections, align the edge of the tape that will establish the paint line. Press down firmly on the edge of the tape that faces the side where you'll be painting.

Remove tape at a moderate rate. If you pull too fast, the tape may shred; if you pull too slowly, you may remove the paint underneath. Start by pulling the tape at a 45-degree angle to the surface. If that leaves adhesive residue behind, slow down and raise the angle, so that you are pulling the tape at a 90-degree angle to the wall.

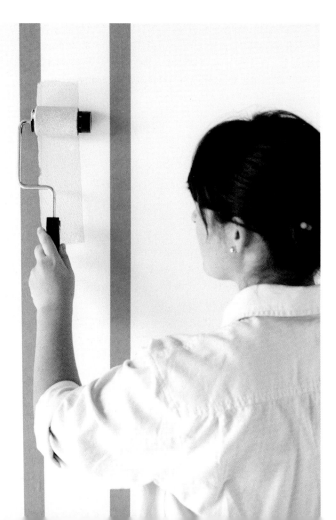

The Eco-Conscious Painter

Are you environmentally conscious? If so, water-based paints are generally the wiser choice because they release far fewer fumes than oil-based paints and are less flammable. However, most water-based formulas still contain small amounts of solvents that can trigger allergic reactions when inhaled, or dry out your skin with prolonged exposure. Always read the material safety data sheet (MSDS), which you can find online, and look for low-odor products that are low in VOCs (volatile organic compounds), with certification from an independent organization such as Green Seal. Avoid products with the words "warning" or "caution" on the label or with hazardous ingredients listed on the MSDS.

Protect Your Floor and Furniture

Painting is more fun when you're not worried about ruining your carpet or favorite sofa, so cover your furnishings well. For small projects, you can use newspaper. If you're painting a larger surface, use plastic drop cloths, canvas, or paper drop cloths with a plastic layer in the middle.

Get Ready to Prime

Primers are the supporting actors on the paint stage; they grip, hide, and seal, helping decorative paint look better. Although primer is usually white, it can be tinted to help achieve a more even shade in the finish paint. You can skip priming if you are painting over existing paint of the same type, but in most other cases, priming will help you achieve a better look.

When to Prime

Prime when you are going to:

- dramatically change the color of a surface
- cover old glossy paint
- cover old oil paint with latex paint
- paint a surface you just patched
- paint bare wood
- paint new drywall

What Primer to Use

As with paint, all primers are not created alike. Here's how to tell them apart.

Water-based primer. Use this for most projects.

Oil-based primer. Use this if you plan to use oil-based paint. It's also an option for problematic surfaces because it adheres better than some water-based primers.

Shellac-based primer. Use this for priming over problematic or especially slick surfaces, such as laminate or gloss oil paint that you don't want to scuff-sand first because it might contain lead. Shellac-based primer seals especially well, so you can use it before you repaint a surface that is heavily stained. Shellac-based primer is ready to re-coat in just 45 minutes, so you can get started on the decorative paint sooner.

Primer-sealer. Some manufacturers also make a water-based primer called primer-sealer (or adhesion sealer), which performs nearly as well as a shellac-based primer—and doesn't smell as bad while it dries.

Quick Tip: Turn Off the Power

If you are painting a wall with electrical sockets or switches, turn off the power at the circuit box, remove the light switch plates, and cover the sockets or switches with painter's masking tape before painting. Restore power once you've replaced the plates.

« Be sure to prime whenever you are dramatically changing the color of a wall. A tinted primer, as pictured here, is especially useful if you plan to paint a dark color.

» Using the right tools and techniques for your paint job will ensure a polished, professional-looking finish.

Paint Like a Pro

After all the prepping, you're finally ready to paint! Every paint pro has his or her list of best practices—here are our top ten.

1. Set enough time aside. Plan your painting when you can work without interruption. That way, the area you just finished painting will still be wet when you paint the next section, allowing the paint to merge together. If you get interrupted, and paint in one area dries before you paint the next section, you are likely to see the overlap, especially if you are using a fairly glossy paint.

2. Read labels. Always read product labels and follow manufacturer's recommendations. All the little details about temperature, prep steps, and time between coats are there for a reason.

3. Dampen your brush or roller with water. Do this before painting and then shake or spin out the excess. Dampening your brush helps keep the paint from drying on the tool and makes it easier to clean afterward.

4. Dip the brush properly. Dip the bristles into the paint no more than one-third of the way and then simply tap the loaded brush (instead of wiping it) against the inside rim of the container a couple of times.

5. Load the roller properly. Fill the paint tray part of the way, and then roll the roller down the tray's corrugated ramp into the paint. Work the roller back and forth over the ramp to distribute the paint evenly onto the roller. Paint shouldn't be dripping off it; nor should there be dry spots.

6. Paint the edges first. When you are painting a large area, begin by painting a band about 2 inches wide around the outside edges. This gets the time-consuming detail work done so that you don't need to slow down once you are painting the main expanse. If you are using matte paint, do all the edges of the room first and then fill in the main expanses. With gloss paint, edge-paint the corners of one section, fill in the main expanse

there, and then move on to the next section. This way, you always have a wet edge and won't see those gloss paint overlaps later.

7. Roll right. For uniform coverage on big areas, work in sections of about 3 feet by 3 feet, first rolling on a N-shaped zigzag and then making a series of up and down passes to even out the paint.

8. Take a combo approach. On furniture, trim, and other woodwork, use a mini roller to apply paint to the surface and then immediately follow with a brush, using the bristles to work paint into corners and details. Smooth out the overall finish with a series of long brushstrokes.

9. Maintain tools while painting. Between coats, keep the painting tools tightly wrapped in plastic rather than rinsing them.

10. Clean tools and store paint. When done, scrape as much paint as you can off tools with a rubber spatula, or wipe rollers and brushes back and forth on newspaper. Then, wash the tools in warm water and a few drops of laundry detergent. If paint has dried on the bristles, comb through them with an old hair comb or a special paintbrush comb. Rinse everything until the water runs clear and let dry. Wipe off the rim of the paint can before you close the container to make sure the lid closes completely.

Let Paint Dry

It's essential to let paint dry completely. Paint may feel dry to the touch after an hour or so, but it takes much longer to actually harden, or "cure," into a tough, plasticlike film. Here's how to achieve a beautiful, durable finish.

Apply thin coats. Thick ones don't cure properly.

Avoid overdoing touch-ups. Excessive touching up keeps the surface film from forming properly. Let the paint dry and *then* apply a second coat if needed.

Read the label for drying time. It might surprise you. Some spray paints can be recoated within an hour or after 24 hours but not in between.

Check the temperature. Make sure the temperature in the house is appropriate for proper paint curing. For most latex paint, the temperature needs to be at least 55 degrees.

Dealing with Lead Paint

If you live in an older home, there's a good chance that some of the painted surfaces contain lead. Lead is toxic, and exposure to lead dust can cause brain damage or health problems, especially in children, and complications for pregnant women. Lead was banned from household paint in 1978, but people continued to use leftover paint for several years. Test for lead with a kit sold at hardware and paint stores. If you have lead-based paint in your home, here's what to do.

• If the paint is in good condition, simply paint over it. Avoid sanding it, as that would stir up dust and release lead into your house.

• If the paint is not in good condition—and it needs to be scraped, sanded, or removed—consider having the painted surface or item replaced (if possible), or hire professionals trained in safely removing lead-based paint.

• If you have to scrape, sand, or remove old paint—and you suspect that it might have lead in it—always wear a NIOSH (National Institute for Occupational Safety and Health)-approved respirator to control lead exposure. Remove the paint in a way that contains the scrapings and doesn't release dust. And then clean up carefully.

For full instructions, contact the National Lead Information Hotline at 1-800-424-LEAD, or log on to *www.epa.gov/lead*

Get to Know Wallcoverings

There's a lot more than paper in most wallpaper these days, which is why the industry now calls it "wallcovering." Be sure to ask at the store whether the style you like is suitable for your project. Here's a guide to some of the terms you'll hear.

Coated and uncoated. A lot of wallpaper is coated with plastic, so it's easy to clean. Vinyl, which is technically polyvinyl chloride, or PVC, is the most common plastic coating. There are other plastic coatings, as well as types that have a sheet of vinyl laminated to the surface. Uncoated wallpaper has no plastic coating and isn't usually washable. Old-fashioned, all-paper wallpaper is in this category, as are many specialty and DIY papers, like the maps (page 116) and the botanical prints (page 113) projects in this book. Don't use a vinyl-coated wallpaper on an exterior wall if you live in a humid climate where you run an air conditioner. The combined hot conditions outside and cool conditions inside can create an environment for mildew.

Quick Tip: Alternates to PVC
PVC contains plasticizers (flexibility agents) that become airborne over time and create a strong plastic odor that people often find objectionable. Some researchers also link PVC to health and environmental problems. If you have concerns about PVC, ask the store for other options.

Unpasted and pre-pasted. Unpasted wallcovering needs wallpaper paste to adhere it to a surface. The labels on the wallcovering and the paste will tell you how to best apply it. Pre-pasted wallcovering comes with adhesive on it; you just add water and wait the recommended time.

Peelable and strippable. Peelable wallpaper has a vinyl-coated layer that can be peeled off. The paper backing, however, needs to be removed with water or wallpaper stripper. Strippable wallpaper can be easily removed—just pull it off, without using any tools, chemicals, or water.

Washable and scrubbable. If a wallcovering is washable, you can gently wipe away smudges using soap and water; with a scrubbable wallcovering, you can really scrub it. If you buy wallpaper that's neither washable nor scrubbable, you can make it easier to clean by brushing or rolling on some clear, matte acrylic after the wallpaper paste dries.

Buy Your Wallcovering

Before you shop, measure the height and width of the surfaces you want to cover, and make a sketch that also shows dimensions of any areas that you won't cover, such as windows or doors. Bring the sketch with you when you shop so a store clerk can check your calculations. Here are a few tips.

Be prepared for inconsistency. Although you'll find pricing based on a single roll, manufacturers produce only double rolls, and they come in different sizes. Be prepared to do some math when figuring out how much you need.

Make sure you buy enough. Be certain you have enough wallcovering to allow for pattern matching across your surface and for full strips from the ceiling to the floor. This typically adds 10 to 20 percent to the amount you think you need.

Consider alternate sources for small projects. Sometimes you need only a little wallpaper, like for wallpapering a desk (page 122) or door panels (page 118). In these cases, consider purchasing from an online company that sells wallpaper by the yard, or ask a store if it sells partially used returned rolls.

Quick Tip: Removing Unpeelable Wallpaper
To remove vinyl unpeelable wallpaper, pepper the paper with holes (using a wallpaper scoring tool), and then sponge or roll on wallpaper stripper, or hot water mixed with a little white vinegar. Wait for the paper to turn dark or to bubble, and then scrape it off.

Products You'll Need

There are only four basic products you'll need for wallcovering.

Primer. Primer under a wallcovering is used to seal the surface so it doesn't suck too much moisture out of the adhesive, and to make removal easier later. Water-based paint primer often works fine for wallcoverings. If you are installing dark wallpaper, use a primer that you can tint to a dark color to help hide gaps.

Sizing. This is a varied product that helps seal or prepare the surface for wallpaper. When you buy wallcovering, ask what type of sizing, if any, you need.

Wallcovering primer with sizing. This is a clear primer made specifically for wallcovering, and it also contains sizing. We recommend this for the projects in this book, but check with the wallcovering store to make sure it is suitable.

Adhesive. If you're buying unpasted paper, buy the adhesive recommended for your wallcovering. Adhesive labeled for use with "all wallcovering types" is always a safe bet.

Know Your Tools

You need only a few specialized tools to install wallpaper and other wallcoverings. Here are the basics.

Wallpaper water tray (for pre-pasted paper only). This long, narrow tray is perfect for submerging pre-pasted wallcoverings in order to dampen and activate the adhesive. A bathtub or a plastic storage bin also works.

Wallpaper paste brush (for unpasted paper only). This short, stout brush is designed to spread adhesive onto large unpasted pieces quickly and with minimum mess. A smaller synthetic-bristle brush is more suitable for small projects.

Wallpaper brush. Thin and wide, with very short bristles, this is used like a squeegee to work bubbles to the edges of sheets of wallpaper after you apply the sheets to the wall.

Wallpaper smoothing tool. This piece of semi-rigid plastic makes firmer contact with the paper than does a brush, so it's better for pressing down small pieces firmly.

Seam roller. This is a tool for going over edges of wallpaper sheets 15 minutes after you install them. On small projects, you can just use the wallpaper smoothing tool, or even a finger.

Taping knife. This large putty knife is helpful when you want to crease wallpaper at room corners (to trim the paper neatly).

Wallpaper sponge. This sponge has small pores and is perfect for cleaning stray adhesive from the surface of the wallpaper.

In addition, make sure you have a ladder or step stool, a carpenter's level or plumb bob, a scissors, and a razor.

Wallpaper Like a Pro

After you've chosen your wallpaper, it's time to apply it. Here are our top five tips for making your projects shine.

1. Ask questions. Be sure to ask the store what installation products and methods to use; what works for one kind of wallcovering might not work for a different one. If your wallcovering needs to be installed differently than what is suggested here, alter the project directions as needed.

2. Remember to prime. This will prevent the wallpaper from peeling (or adhering too tightly when you want to remove it).

3. Establish a plumb line. If you're wallpapering a wall or a room, always use a carpenter's level or a plumb bob on a string to establish a line that's perfectly vertical. Every two or three sheets, check again to make sure things are still even.

4. Give yourself wiggle room. Except when you're wallpapering small areas, such as stair risers or door panels, avoid cutting sheets to the exact lengths you need. Allow 2 inches extra at the top and bottom, and then trim the sheets in place. This allows you to accommodate ceilings or floors that aren't level.

5. Buy extra. Remember that you'll need extra wallpaper so you can match the pattern. The longer the distance between the repeats of the pattern, the more allowance you'll need.

Get to Know Fabric

Transforming your home with colorful fabric opens up another whole universe of materials, tools, and techniques. Here's what to think about.

Fabric type. Home decor fabrics tend to be a little wider and heftier than clothing fabrics. They often have a coating that resists soiling and adds a little shine and stiffness. Washing may remove this coating, leaving the fabric limp and dull. So if you are sewing something that you plan to launder, clothing or quilting fabric may be a better choice. Decor fabric works well for things that don't need laundering, though.

Patterns. Solid-color fabrics or random prints are easiest for beginning sewers because mistakes won't be as evident. With a geometric pattern like stripes, it's easier to see if the seams are off. Plaids are the most complicated of all because the design needs to line up vertically and horizontally.

Quick Tip: Get Pinking

To keep an unhemmed fabric edge from fraying, cut the edge with pinking shears. This will create a zigzag edge. Threads at the tips will still fray, but they're very short, so the overall edge will stay intact.

Weight. Heavyweight fabrics tend to be the most durable, but they're not always the best bet because home sewing machines may not be able to pierce through layers of thick fabric.

Stretchability. For most home decor projects, the best fabric is one that does not easily stretch. Avoid knits, and focus on woven fabrics. Before you buy, test a few fabrics you like by tugging a corner lengthwise, crosswise, and at a 45-degree angle. The less the shape changes, the easier the fabric will be to sew.

Know Your Tools

Only a few tools are needed for sewing. Here's the short list.

Needles. Whether you are sewing by hand or machine, choose a thin needle for sewing lightweight fabric and a thick needle for sewing bulkier fabric. For general-purpose hand-sewing, use a "sharp"—a needle of medium length with a small, rounded eye. If you will be making a lot of tiny stitches, use a "between." Embroidery needles, which are long and have an oval eye, are helpful for making long stitches or when using thick thread. For machine sewing, match the tip shape to the type of fabric and the eye size to the type of thread.

Thread. If you want stitches to blend in to the fabric color, choose a thread color that is slightly darker than the main color of the fabric. If you're combining patterns, choose a thread color that is common to both. Either cotton or polyester thread is fine for the projects in this book.

Scissors. Use bent-handle scissors with long blades for cutting fabric; for clipping threads, a smaller scissors is better. Get scissors resharpened if they become dull.

Sewing machine. Although it's possible to sew anything with just a needle and thread (tailors did it for generations!), you'll get more uniform stitches and save time with a sewing machine. All the projects in this book can be accomplished by hand-sewing, though a sewing machine is recommended for the sink skirt (page 153) and the fabric footrest (page 156).

Sew Like a Pro

Now that you know the basics, it's time to get sewing—here are our top five pieces of advice.

1. Check the design. If you are using a fabric with a print, make sure the design is on grain, meaning that it runs parallel to the selvages (the woven-in borders).

2. Square up fabric. If you buy fabric with a woven-in pattern (stripes, checks, or a plaid), cut across the fabric along one line of the pattern close to one end. Then fold the fabric in half so the selvage edges are stacked. If both layers at the cut edge don't line up, stretch the fabric as needed to square it up.

3. Make tight, even stitches. A neat job requires stitches that are all about the same length with the thread pulled just enough so the pieces hold tightly together but don't pucker. If you're hand-sewing and see puckers, use a needle or a blunt part of a seam ripper to retract the thread a few stitches back, easing the tension. If you're sewing by machine, stop sewing and adjust the stitch length or the thread or bobbin tension. Ease the tension on the previous stitching by working the gathers toward the place where you stopped stitching. Then resume stitching, starting an inch or so back from where you left off.

4. Press as you go. Whenever you create a seam that you'll later cross with another seam, press open the first seam allowance (the ½ inch or so between the fabric edges and the stitching), or press the seam allowance to one side. Do this before you stitch the second seam so it will lie flat. You can use an iron to do this or, with some fabrics, just apply finger pressure.

5. Make a test sample. If instructions seem confusing, especially when they involve a lot of folding or turning inside out, try out the procedures on scrap fabric or even scrap paper, and use tape or staples instead of stitching.

Enjoy the Journey

It can be easy to become so focused on doing things right—or getting them done quickly—that projects feel more like labor than enjoyment. Remember that mistakes are par for the course and above all, have fun!

» With the right instructions and tools, recovering chairs with your favorite fabric pattern is simple—even for a novice sewer.

3

Transform rooms with paint

Who doesn't love paint? With a couple of cans of color and some rollers and brushes, you can take a room from dingy to dazzling in the space of a weekend—and sometimes less. This chapter will show you how to create a chic tricolor wall, transform a fireplace, and paint a unique blackboard wall. The sweetest part: If you change your mind about a color later on, all you have to do is repaint.

Two-toned Wall »

Bring the sky into your bathroom by painting the walls a mixture of soft blue and white. For extra cheerfulness, hang a mirror from a pretty piece of fabric attached to a wood board.

Kitchen Doodling ≫

A kitchen is a great place for a chalkboard wall (see page 58)—you can write notes here about grocery shopping, recipes, and daily to-dos.

Brilliant Color »

If you have a room with a lot of natural light, paint it a deep color like the teal pictured here. Think a strong color might over-whelm the space? Paint only one wall that color and leave the other three white or cream. To learn how, see page 50.

(\$) (\$)

Entire room makeover

Nothing transforms a room as quickly or as economically as paint. Adding fresh color can instantly brighten a sterile kitchen, calm a hectic living room, or bring new life to your weary den.

First-Timer Tip

On rectangular ceilings, paint across the shorter dimension so that section of the ceiling won't dry before you start the next. This will make the transition between sections look more even.

Style Note

Not sure what finish to choose for your walls? Matte will offer a depth of color, whereas eggshell or semi-gloss will allow more light (and candlelight!) to reflect off the walls. See page 23 for more on finishes.

Materials

- patch material (see page 26)
- wall texture spray (for textured walls that need patching)
- primer
- matte latex paint for ceiling, 1 quart per 100 square feet
- any sheen of latex paint for walls, 1 gallon per 350 square feet
- gloss or semi-gloss latex enamel for trim, 1 quart per 100 square feet

Tools

- drop cloths, ladder or step stool
- microfiber dust cloth,
- two or three safety pins
- broom or dust mop
- rubber gloves, bucket, and sponge
- household cleaner, or deglosser if existing paint has a gloss finish
- putty knife
- sandpaper or sanding sponge, 180 grit and coarser, as needed (see step 2)
- vacuum
- paint tray
- roller, 9 inch, preferably with an extendable handle (for ceiling)
- synthetic-bristle brush, 1½ inch or 2 inch
- painter's masking tape, 1 inch or wider

continued on page 46

Steps

1. Prep

Clear the room except for heavy furniture; push that to the center. Cover the furniture and the floor with the drop cloths. Shut off power at the circuit breaker. Use a circuit tester to make sure the power is off, then remove the switch covers and ceiling fixture(s) if necessary. Clean cobwebs and lint from the ceiling, walls, and top edges of the trim with the dust cloth pinned around the broom or dust mop. Wearing gloves, wash the trim, cabinets, and doors with water and the cleaner or deglosser. Wash the walls, too, if they are very dirty or in a kitchen or bathroom. (If the paint is spattered with oil or other grime, you may need a more powerful cleaner, such as TSP. Check the primer label for suggestions.)

2. Patch

With the putty knife, use the patch material to fill any gouges. Let dry. Sand the patches flat; start with 100 grit, then go to 150 grit. On woodwork, make a final pass with 180 grit. Vacuum up the sanding residue. If the walls are textured, apply wall texture spray to any patches.

3. Prime

If you are priming only the patches, use the synthetic-bristle brush to apply the primer. If you are priming the entire surface (see page 28 for when to prime), prime in the same manner that you'll be painting each section of the room, as detailed below. Let primer dry.

4. Paint the ceiling

Apply a band of matte latex paint about 2 inches wide to the ceiling edges. Make sure the paint reaches all the way into the corners, even if some gets onto the walls. Then pour some of the same paint into the paint tray, and use the roller to fill in the main expanse of the ceiling. Progress across the ceiling in relatively straight lines. Let dry. Reinstall the ceiling fixtures.

5. Mask the walls

Unless the wall paint matches the ceiling paint, apply the painter's masking tape on the ceiling close to where it meets the walls. Also tape off any trim or other surfaces that you won't be painting. Press the tape firmly down on the edge that faces the surfaces you are painting.

6. Paint the walls

Paint the walls with the latex paint, working in sections about 3 feet wide. In the first section, use the brush to paint a band about 2 inches wide along the top of the wall. Do the same at the base of the wall. Then pour some wall paint into the paint tray and fill in the top half of that wall section by rolling a thick N shape onto the wall, then evening out the paint by rolling up and down through the N in straight lines. Paint the lower area in the same way. Finish by running the roller (without reloading it with paint) from the top of the wall to the bottom in a single pass. At the corners, switch to the brush. Complete the rest of the sections on that wall. Paint the remaining walls in the same way. When you are painting the second wall of each corner, pull the paint back horizontally so you don't leave drips or smear the wall you just painted. If the paint looks thin or blotchy after it dries, add a second coat. Once the paint dries, remove the tape. Reinstall the switch covers and restore the power.

7. Paint the trim and cabinets

With the brush and the latex enamel, paint the window interiors first (page 52). Then paint the window trim (page 52). If you're in a hurry to use the room, you can move back most of the furnishings and take your time painting the doors and cabinets (pages 60 and 62).

$

Painted fireplace

Flames dancing in a fireplace always look inviting—as should the bricks that surround them. If your fireplace is looking dingy, update it with paint.

Materials
- acrylic masonry primer for interior use
- latex paint, 1 quart per 70 square feet

Tools
- vacuum
- rubber gloves, bucket, and sponge
- household cleaner
- painter's masking tape, 1 inch or wider
- drop cloths
- ladder or step stool
- paint tray
- mini roller
- synthetic-bristle brush, 2½ inch

Style Note
To create an effect similar to what masons achieve with a blend of brick colors, use several shades of one color and apply them randomly to individual bricks.

Steps

1. Clean
Vacuum the brick surrounding the firebox. Don't vacuum the brick inside the firebox, since vacuuming there can be a fire hazard. If there is soot or efflorescence on the bricks, put on gloves and scrub it away with water and the cleaner. Rinse thoroughly, and let the surface dry for a day.

2. Tape
Apply the painter's masking tape to protect any wall, floor, or ceiling surfaces next to the brick.

3. Prime
Position the drop cloth. Pour some primer into the tray. Starting at the top, use the roller to prime the brick in sections about 2 feet wide and several feet high. Roll back and forth and diagonally. Follow with the synthetic-bristle brush to fill in gaps and remove drips. As you complete each section, brush horizontally across the face of the bricks to even out the primer.

4. Paint
Apply the latex paint in the same way as the primer. Let dry, then apply a second coat. When that is dry, remove the tape.

First-Timer Tip

Do this project only if you're certain about it; once you apply paint to brick, there's no easy way to take it off!

$

Decorative trim

Think of trim as a room's jewelry—the finishing touch that sets the style, adds a little flair, and pulls different elements together. Create a statement with your trim by painting it a color that contrasts with the rest of the room. It will make the different features pop and completely change the look of the space.

Materials
- wood filler (if needed)
- primer (if needed)
- gloss or semi-gloss latex enamel

Tools
- drop cloths
- ladder or step stool
- painter's masking tape, 1 inch or wider
- putty knife (to apply wood filler)
- rubber gloves, bucket, and sponge
- household cleaner, or deglosser if existing paint has a gloss finish
- sandpaper or sanding sponge, 180 grit
- microfiber dust cloth
- synthetic-bristle brush, 1 inch to 2 inch, preferably angled

Steps

1. Prep
Move the furniture and any area rugs away from the walls, and take down any window treatments that are next to or underneath any trim you will be painting. Position the drop cloths. Apply the painter's masking tape to protect the surrounding surfaces, and press down firmly along all edges facing the trim. Using the putty knife and wood filler, patch any holes or dents in the trim.

2. Wash and scuff
Wearing gloves, wash the trim with water and the cleaner or deglosser. When the surface is dry, lightly scuff up the paint with the sandpaper or sanding sponge, and wipe away the residue with the dust cloth.

3. Prime
Using the brush, brush primer over any patches. If there is oil paint on the trim (see page 30 for how to check) or if you are switching between light and dark colors, you need to prime all the trim. Apply the primer with the brush, taking care to get into all the curved surfaces. Complete each piece of trim before you go on to the next. Let dry.

4. Paint
Apply the latex enamel with the brush, using the same method described in step 3. To ensure a smooth coat on trim pieces that are too long to paint in one stroke (especially if you are working on a ladder), begin painting at one end or corner and gradually lift up on the brush as you complete the stroke. Begin the next stroke a workable distance beyond the end of the first stroke, and brush toward the first section you painted. After the overlap, gradually lift up on the brush. Continue in this manner until you have painted the entire trim piece. Then go on to the next piece.

5. Recoat
Inspect the paint. If you see gaps, apply a second coat. Do not apply a second coat unless it is needed, though, since too many layers of paint will eventually obscure the trim's details.

Style Note

If you have trim with lots of detail that you want to emphasize, paint it with a gloss finish and the ceiling and walls with a matte finish. If you want to tone down trim details, paint everything in a cohesive matte finish.

$

Bright accent wall

If you've been itching to paint a wild, bright color but don't want to over-whelm the room, paint an accent wall. It's like adding just the right amount of spice to a meal. The best wall to accent: The one where your eye naturally wants to go.

Materials
- primer
- any sheen of brightly colored latex paint, 1 quart per 100 square feet

Tools
- drop cloths
- ladder or step stool
- microfiber dust cloth
- rubber gloves, bucket, and sponge
- household cleaner, or deglosser if existing paint has a gloss finish
- painter's masking tape, 1 inch or wider
- synthetic-bristle brush, 1½ inch or 2 inch
- paint tray
- roller, 9 inch
- artist's brush

Steps

1. Clean
Position the drop cloths. Wipe the accent wall and the top of the baseboard with the dust cloth. If the wall is dirty—or if it's in a bathroom or kitchen—put on gloves and wash the wall with water and the cleaner or deglosser.

2. Tape
Apply the painter's masking tape to the ceiling, baseboard, and walls on both sides, just beyond the accent wall edges. Press down firmly on the tape edges that face the accent wall.

3. Patch and prime
If you need to patch, see instructions on page 46. Then, prime the patches using the synthetic-bristle brush. If you are priming the entire surface (see page 28 for when to prime), use the brush to apply a band of primer about 2 inches wide along the taped edges, directing the brush away from the tape. Next, pour primer into the paint tray. With the roller, prime the main expanse of the accent wall, working on sections about 3 feet across at a time. First, prime the top of each section by rolling on primer in an N shape. Then roll vertically to even out the primer. In the same way, prime the lower part of the section. Finally, run the nearly dry roller from the top of the wall to the bottom. Go over the primer only once this way, then let it dry.

4. Paint
Apply the latex paint to the wall, using the same procedure you used in step 3, but paint edges in sections as you progress across the wall. After you roll from the top of the wall to the bottom in each area, avoid going back to touch up areas that look thin. Let dry.

5. Touch up and complete
If the paint looks thin or blotchy when dry, add a second coat. Let the paint dry again. Then remove the tape carefully. With the artist's brush, touch up any places where paint seeped under the tape or the tape pulled away the paint.

Style Note

For a sleek look, balance the brightly colored accent wall with a deep, grounded color on a piece of furniture or on the window frames, as pictured here.

$

Painted windows

Painting double-hung windows can be tricky because of hard-to-reach parts. Here's an easy way to do a beautiful job.

Materials

- lightweight spackle
- primer (if needed)
- gloss or semi-gloss latex enamel

Tools

- drop cloth
- ladder or step stool
- screwdriver
- paint scraper
- damp cloth
- rubber gloves, bucket, and sponge
- cleaning cloth
- bleach (if existing paint is stained)
- household cleaner, or deglosser if existing paint has a gloss finish
- sandpaper or sanding sponge, 180 grit
- putty knife (if you spackle)
- microfiber dust cloth
- painter's masking tape, 1 inch or wider
- angled synthetic-bristle brush, 1 inch to 1½ inch
- double-edge razor blade

Steps

1. Prep
Remove any window coverings. With the screwdriver, remove window hardware. Position the drop cloth. With the paint scraper, remove any loose paint.

2. Clean and scuff
With the damp cloth, wipe off mildew from the window frames and trim. Wearing gloves, remove stains with a solution of 3 parts water to 1 part bleach. Rinse well. Then, wash the paint with water and the cleaner or deglosser; let dry. Lightly scuff up the paint with the sandpaper or sanding sponge. Wipe with the dust cloth. (Caution: Do not mix bleach with any cleaner that contains ammonia, and avoid getting deglosser on the glass.)

3. Patch and mask
Using the putty knife, fill any small holes in the wood with spackle. Apply the tape to the glass and to the wall surrounding the window. Press the tape down firmly along the edges where you will paint. At the corners of the glass, press the putty knife over the tape, then neatly tear off the tape along the knife edge.

4. Prime
Brush primer over any bare spots or spackle patches. If the old paint is oil based (see page 30 for how to check), prime the entire surface, following the procedure in step 5. Let dry.

5. Paint the sash
Lower the upper sash. Then raise the lower sash so you can reach the bottom edge of the upper sash, and paint the surface that faces the room but is concealed when the window is closed. Then close both window sections most of the way and paint the remaining surfaces that face the room, as well as the top edge of the bottom sash. (Don't paint the top edge of the top sash and the bottom edge of the bottom sash). Leave the sash slightly ajar while the paint dries.

6. Paint the remaining parts
Paint the molding (be careful not to get paint in the recesses) and then paint the window trim from top to bottom. Remove the tape. Use the razor blade to remove any paint that has seeped onto the glass.

Alternate Method

If you are painting windows framed with vinyl or aluminum, the procedure is different. Wash vinyl with a TSP substitute; wash aluminum with a little vinegar. Then, use a water-based primer suitable for slick surfaces and latex enamel as the finish paint.

Maintenance Tip

To keep your newly painted window(s) from sticking, rub a little mineral oil on the molding edge facing the window, and open and close the window daily for the first month.

$ $

Tricolor wall

Nothing brings a room together like breaking things up a bit. This tricolor wall will make any room cohesive, stylish, and one of a kind.

Materials

- primer
- latex paint in three colors (one bold and two neutral), 1 quart per 100 square feet

Tools

- drop cloths
- ladder or step stool
- paint tray
- roller, 9 inch or mini
- pencil
- painter's masking tape, 1 inch or wider
- synthetic-bristle brush, 1½ inch or 2 inch
- carpenter's level

First-Timer Tip

Right after step 4, brush a little of the top color paint along the edge of the tape that faces the bottom portion of the wall, and let it dry. The paint will seep into any gaps and plug them, leaving no room for the second color to sneak in there when you paint the bottom portion of the wall.

Steps

1. Design the wall

Decide which three colors you'll use for the tricolor wall and how you'll use them. Two colors will be on the wall; one color will be for accessories. (The other three walls in the room should be painted one of these three colors. If they aren't already, paint them first, referring to the instructions on page 46.)

2. Prep, prime, and tape

Position the drop cloths. Prep, and prime the wall (if you didn't in step 1), following the instructions on page 46. Let dry. Apply the painter's masking tape to the ceiling and baseboard, as well as to the flanking walls (except in places where the color will not change from wall to wall). Press the tape down firmly on the edges that face the wall that will be painted.

3. Paint the top of the wall

With the pencil, mark a rough line on the two-color wall a little below where you want the colors to change. With the brush, paint a band about 2 inches wide at the top of the wall. Pour some paint into the tray. Use the roller to paint the rest of the top section of the wall, painting a little below the rough color-change line. Remove the tape at the ceiling and sides of the upper part of the wall. Wipe off any paint that seeped under the tape. Let dry.

4. Establish the color-change line

Use the carpenter's level and a pencil to mark a horizontal line precisely where the colors will change. Apply tape on the newly painted surface just above that line. Press the tape down firmly on the edges that face the unpainted portion of the wall.

5. Paint the bottom of the wall

Using the same procedure you used in step 3, paint the lower part of the wall with the second paint color. Remove the existing tape. If any paint seeped under the tape, wipe it off. Let dry.

6. Add the third color

Use the third color to paint a shelf that will hang on the duotone wall (as pictured here), the trim (see page 48), or a chair or a bookcase that will sit near or against the wall.

Style Note

If you need a little help selecting your tricolor palette, check out these four ideas:

Golden gate: Relaxed orange, warm off-white, faded taupe

Mountain spring: Orchid, pistachio white, mossy green

High desert: Coral, light mauve, smoky mauve

Southland retro: Light jade, cool white, coal blue

Style Note

The palette pictured here is called Cascada; it consists of peacock blue, cool slate, and pale gray.

Ⓢ

Painted bookcase

Bookcases are for more than storing your library. Paint the cubbyholes in vibrant colors, and you'll also have a display case for knickknacks, art, and photographs.

Materials

- six colors of latex paint, sample sizes

Tools

- drop cloth
- sandpaper or sanding sponge, 180 grit
- damp rag
- painter's masking tape, as wide as the cubbyhole edges
- synthetic-bristle brush, 1½ inch or 2 inch

Alternate Method

Add color to your bookcase interior without painting: Cut foam core board to fit the back of each cubbyhole, and cover the boards with colored fabric. Then pop each insert into place, using double-sided tape if necessary for hold.

Steps

1. Scuff

Position the drop cloth. Assuming that the bookcase is painted and you want to leave the exterior as is, begin by scuffing up the cubbyhole interiors with the sandpaper or sanding sponge. Wipe away the residue with the damp rag. (If you want to paint the rest of the bookcase first, see page 63.) Let dry.

2. Tape

Apply painter's masking tape to the front edges of the cubbyholes. Press the tape down firmly along the edges where you will be painting.

3. Paint

With the brush, paint the cubbyholes, working on one at a time. Paint the top surface first, and then—in this order—the back, sides, and bottom. To keep from smearing paint at the corners, use the brush to pull paint from each corner toward the center of that surface. Once you finish a section, avoid retouching the paint for now, even if you see messy areas, but do lightly brush away any drips. Repeat for all the cubbyholes. (For efficiency, paint all sections that will be one color before you switch to the next color.) Remove the tape. With the damp rag, wipe off any paint that bled under the tape. Let dry.

4. Touch up and complete

With the brush, touch up any gaps. If the paint looks thin or blotchy when dry, tape the edges as needed and then add a second coat.

Style Note

For a multidimensional look, paint the backs of each cubbyhole with one color, and the top, bottom, and sides with a second color. Paint the back first and, when that dries, tape around its edges and paint the other surfaces.

Chalkboard wall

Create an erasable chalkboard wall for grocery lists, notes, and good ol' doodling.

Materials

- drywall topping mix (if the wall is textured)
- primer
- chalkboard paint, 1 quart per 100 square feet
- white chalk

Tools

- drop cloth
- ladder or step stool
- microfiber dust cloth
- rubber gloves, bucket, and sponge
- household cleaner, or deglosser if existing paint has a gloss finish
- painter's masking tape, 1 inch or wider
- taping knives, 6 inch and 10 inch
- disposable respirator for sanding dust
- sandpaper, 120 grit and 150 grit
- vacuum
- synthetic-bristle brush, 2 inch
- paint tray
- roller, 9 inch
- chalkboard eraser

First-Timer Tip
Chalkboard paint adheres to many surfaces such as wood, metal, masonry, drywall, plaster, glass, and concrete. If you want to draw fine details on your chalkboard, choose a smooth surface.

▶ Steps

1. Prep
Position the drop cloth. If the wall looks clean, simply dust it with the dust cloth. If the wall needs to be cleaned, put on gloves and wash the wall with water and the cleaner or deglosser. Wipe away residue and let dry.

2. Tape
To avoid smearing chalkboard paint on adjacent surfaces, apply the painter's masking tape to the ceiling, baseboard, and flanking walls. Place the tape just beyond the chalkboard wall. Press down firmly on the tape edges that face the chalkboard wall.

3. Smooth
If the wall has a textured surface, apply the drywall topping mix. Mix it with water to a creamy consistency. With the narrower taping knife, apply a thin layer to the wall by making vertical passes with the knife. As you complete each section, quickly smooth the area with the wider knife. Don't worry if you leave ridges. Let the mix on the wall dry completely (this could take 24 hours). Then knock off the ridges by scraping the smaller knife across the wall. Put on the disposable respirator and sand the surface smooth starting with 120-grit sandpaper and finishing with 150-grit. Vacuum the wall and floor.

4. Prime
With the synthetic-bristle brush, apply a 2-inch-wide band of primer along the perimeter of the wall. Pour primer into the paint tray and use the roller to fill in the rest of the surface. Working in sections about 3 feet wide, roll a thick N shape onto the top half of the wall and distribute the primer by rolling vertically through it. Then prime the lower part of the wall in the same way. Finally, smooth the primer by rolling in one pass from the top of the wall to the bottom. Let dry.

5. Paint
Apply the chalkboard paint in the same way that you applied the primer. Let dry. Apply a second coat after waiting as long as the manufacturer's label specifies.

6. Condition
Wait several days for the paint to cure. Then, with the side of a piece of chalk, rub the entire surface of the chalkboard paint to condition it (this makes it easier to clean later on). Erase the chalk, and use your chalkboard. You can wipe down your chalkboard with a moist cloth to keep it clean, but wait at least four days after conditioning it to do so.

Alternate Method
Don't want to paint an entire wall? Use the same process on a piece of hardboard, and hang it like a picture.

Style Note
You can paint chalkboards in colors other than black and green—just buy a tint base and ask the paint store to add the color you want. For a custom color, make your own chalkboard paint by mixing two tablespoons of unsanded tile grout per one cup of matte latex paint.

($)

Colorful panel doors

A little paint can do a lot for your panel doors, taking them from utilitarian fixtures to major decorative accents.

Materials

- primer (if needed)
- gloss or semi-gloss latex enamel

Tools

- drop cloth
- rubber gloves, bucket, and sponge-type scrub pad
- household cleaner, or deglosser if existing paint has a gloss finish
- sandpaper or sanding sponge, 180 grit
- vacuum
- painter's masking tape, 1 inch or wider
- screwdriver
- synthetic-bristle brush, 2 inch or 2½ inch
- mini roller
- paint tray

▶ Steps

1. Prep the surface
Check that any existing paint on the door is intact and not flaking off. (If it is flaking, you'll need to get the door stripped first or the new paint will peel.) Position the drop cloth. If the door is painted, put on gloves and wash the door with water and the cleaner or deglosser. Let dry, and then lightly scuff up the paint with the sandpaper or sanding sponge, but avoid sanding through the paint. Vacuum.

2. Prep the hardware
Cover the door hinges with the painter's masking tape. With the screwdriver, remove the doorknob, or leave it in place and mask it, too. The latter approach is safer on an old door because the knob assembly may be tricky to reinstall.

3. Prime the door
If there is oil-based paint on the door (see page 30 for how to check), or if you are switching from a dark to a light color, you need to prime. Apply the primer using the same procedure described for the latex paint in steps 4, 5, and 6 below.

4. Paint the outer edges
With the brush, apply the paint to the outer edges of the door, except at the bottom. When you are done with each edge, run the nearly dry brush along the corners to smooth out any drips.

5. Paint the panels
Pour some paint into the tray. Work on one panel at a time. Brush paint around the bevel, and then, with the roller, apply paint to the main part of the panel. Go over the paint immediately with a series of long, side-by-side brush strokes. Paint the other panels the same way.

6. Paint the door frame
Brush the paint around the doorknob, if it's still in place. Then paint the frames surrounding the panels, using the same roller and brush combination as in step 5. If there is a flat section at the center, paint it first. Paint the top horizontal piece next, then paint the verticals down as far as the next horizontal. Then, paint the next horizontal. Work your way down the door in this fashion. Repeat steps 5 and 6 on the other side of the door. Let dry.

7. Touch up and complete
If the paint looks thin or blotchy when dry, touch up any gaps with the brush or add a second coat.

Alternate Method
Remove the door before you paint. It's trickier to do, but it reduces the risk of drips and allows you to take off the hinges for cleaning or refinishing.

Style Note
If a door connects two rooms, paint each side of the door to match the room it faces when it's closed. Remember, though, that when a door is open, its "inside" face looks out on the other room, so choose colors with that in mind.

Cabinet makeover

No matter what type of cabinets you have, you can create a whole new look by simply repainting them.

Materials

- wood filler
- primer for slick surfaces
- gloss or semi-gloss latex paint or latex enamel, 1 quart per 50 square feet (to allow two coats)

Tools

- drop cloths
- ladder or step stool (if needed)
- painter's masking tape, 1 inch or wider
- screwdriver
- pencil
- spacer blocks
- rubber gloves, bucket, and sponge
- household cleaner, or deglosser if existing paint has a gloss finish
- putty knife
- sandpaper or sanding sponge, 100 grit and 180 grit
- microfiber dust cloth
- paint tray
- mini roller
- synthetic-bristle brush, 2 inch or 2½ inch

▶ Steps

1. Prep

Clear off the counters and position the drop cloths. Apply the painter's masking tape to the adjoining walls. Press down firmly on the side facing the cabinets. Remove the cabinet drawers. Remove the doors, using the screwdriver to take off the hinges. Also remove the knobs and handles. As you work, use the pencil to number all the doors and drawers and their corresponding locations in the cabinet. Make these notations in places that won't be painted, such as hinge recesses or drawer bottoms. Then place the cabinet doors on the spacer blocks, on another drop cloth. Wearing gloves, wash the surfaces you'll paint with water and the cleaner or deglosser. Wipe away all residue. Let dry.

2. Smooth the surfaces

With the putty knife, press wood filler into any nicks. When the filler dries, sand the patches smooth with the 100-grit sand-paper or sanding sponge. With the 180-grit sandpaper or sanding sponge, scuff all the surfaces. Remove all residue with the dust cloth.

3. Prime

Pour the primer into the paint tray. Working on one section or surface at a time, use the roller to apply the primer to the pre-pared surface and then immediately use the brush to get the primer into corners and to remove excess paint from the edges. Finally, brush one more time over the primer, using long strokes side by side. Brush horizontally on the drawer fronts and vertically on the cabinets and the door panels; on the framing around the panels, brush in the long direction of the wood. Let dry.

4. Paint

Apply the finish paint in the same way you applied the primer. Don't worry if you see ridges from the brush marks; they will flatten as the paint dries. After the first coat dries, apply a second coat. Let dry.

5. Finish

Reattach the handles and knobs. Replace the drawers and doors. (If you don't have hinges that come apart, it's usually easiest to attach the hinges to the doors first, and then screw them back onto the cabinets.)

Style Note

Are you forever banging your head when the upper cabinet doors are open? If so, simply remove them, as pictured here. Before you prime, patch the cabinet to smooth over screw holes or recesses that were cut for hinges. Save the doors in case you change your mind later.

First-Timer Tips

» To prevent the cabinet doors from sticking after you paint, rub a little furniture wax along the mating edges or attach clear door protectors to the backs of the doors.

» If you want new cabinet hardware, buy it before you begin repainting. If the new hardware needs different screw holes than the old hardware did, plug the old holes while you prep the cabinets.

$ $

Painted stair runner

Give your stairs a multilayered look with a fun, painted stair runner.

Materials

- wood filler
- primer for slick surfaces
- gloss latex enamel (for skirt boards, handrail, etc.), 1 quart
- gloss or matte latex porch and floor paint, four colors (2 for risers, 2 for treads), 1 quart each

Tools

- rubber gloves, bucket, and sponge
- household cleaner, or deglosser if existing paint has a gloss finish
- putty knife
- sandpaper or sanding sponge, 100 grit and 180 grit
- vacuum
- painter's masking tape, 1 inch or wider
- drop cloths
- paint tray
- mini roller
- synthetic-bristle brush, 1½ inch or 2 inch
- pencil
- ruler and drafting triangle

Steps

1. Prep

Wearing gloves, wash the stairs with water and the cleaner or deglosser. Let dry. Use the putty knife to press wood filler into any holes. When the patches are dry, sand them with the coarser sandpaper or sanding sponge. Then switch to the finer grit to scuff up all surfaces. Vacuum.

2. Prime

Apply tape to the handrail brackets and the walls next to the surfaces you will paint. Press the tape down toward the side to be painted. Position the drop cloths. Pour the primer into the tray and use the roller to prime the handrails, the skirt boards, and any other trim you like. In each area, immediately follow with the brush to get the primer into corners and to smooth the surface. Prime the stairs in the same way, starting at the top and moving down.

3. Paint the trim

Use the same method as in step 2 to apply the gloss latex enamel to the handrail, skirt boards, and other trim. Let dry.

4. Mark the runner

Design your runner to stop 5 to 7 inches from each side of the stairway. Using the pencil, mark the runner borders on the risers and treads. Use the ruler and the drafting triangle to keep the lines straight. The line on each tread should be at a right angle to the line on the preceding riser.

5. Paint the side colors

Starting at the top of the staircase, paint the side sections of the risers. When the paint dries, apply masking tape to the top and bottom edges of the riser sections you just painted. Redraw any lines you painted over, using the lines still visible on the treads as a guide. Then paint the edges of the treads. Remove the tape.

6. Paint the runner

Using the lines on the risers as your guide, apply new tape just outside the lines that show the runner on the treads and risers. Using the same procedure as in step 5, paint the runner on the risers. Let dry. Then paint the runner on the treads. Remove the tape. Let dry.

First-Timer Tips

» If you must use the stairs while the paint is wet, paint only every other tread and let people walk on the unpainted steps (adhere sticky notes to guide them). When the paint dries, finish the remaining treads.

» Gloss paint is easier to wipe clean than matte paint, but dust shows less on matte paint. So choose the sheen that will work best for your stairs.

Style Note

Consider coordinating the stair paint with an area rug (as pictured here).

$

Painted tub

A claw-foot tub looks luxurious no matter what, but painting it a bright color gives your bathroom a playful, modern feel.

Materials
- rust-bonding primer (only if there's rust)
- shellac-based primer
- latex enamel, 1 quart

Tools
- drop cloths
- rubber gloves, bucket, and sponge-type scrub pad
- household cleaner, or deglosser if existing paint has a gloss finish
- painter's masking tape, 1 inch or wider
- synthetic-bristle brush, 1½ inch
- paint tray
- mini roller

Style Note
For a classy look, paint the feet a contrasting color. White feet look especially sharp on a tub with a white interior. Metallic paints are another option.

Steps

1. Wash
You'll be painting only the exterior of the tub. Check that any existing exterior paint is intact and not flaking off. (If it is flaking, you'll need to have the tub stripped or sandblasted first so the new paint won't peel.) Position the drop cloths. Wearing gloves, wash the exterior of the tub with water and the cleaner or deglosser. Clean as much of the outside of the tub as you have access to. Let dry.

2. Apply the tape
Apply the painter's masking tape to the top edge of the tub feet or to the floor around the feet, depending on whether you are leaving the feet with their existing finish or are painting them. Also apply tape along the top rim of the tub, to keep the interior paint-free.

3. Treat the rust
Inspect the tub exterior, and the feet if you plan to paint them. If you find rust, use the brush to apply the rust-bonding primer over those areas (this chemically converts the rust so the paint will bond to the surface).

4. Prep and prime the surface
Don't sand, as you normally might before priming, because the existing paint is likely to contain lead. Pour the shellac-based primer into the paint tray, and use the roller to paint the main areas of the tub exterior. Then use the brush to smooth out the finish and fill in where the roller won't reach, such as the underside of the tub rim. Prime the feet, too, if you plan to paint them.

5. Paint the exterior and feet
Apply the latex enamel in the same way you applied the primer. (Skip the feet if you'll paint them a contrasting color—see Style Note.) When the first coat dries, apply a second coat if needed. Let dry.

First-Timer Tips

» If you need to paint a tub that is close to a wall, wear long rubber gloves when reaching between the wall and tub (to protect your arm from paint) and consider using a sponge to apply the paint.

» Don't worry if you leave gaps along a tub edge that you can't see. The paint is just for show, so gaps you can't see don't matter.

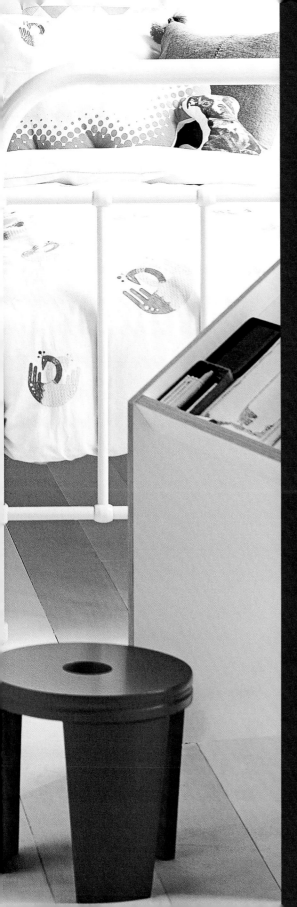

4

Create effects with paint

Paint doesn't only change the look of an entire room; it can be used to create all kinds of detailed effects on your walls, floors, furniture, and window coverings. Here, you'll learn how to paint eye-catching designs—including stripes, chevron patterns, and accent blocks—all over your house. Blank roller shade? Blasé table? Make them sparkle with a new look. So grab some stencils and fine-point brushes, and let your inner artist out.

Stripe the Wall ⩯

If you love stripes, send them across your walls in both directions, and create this playful look. Keep the carpet or floor a neutral color so the room doesn't look too busy.

Playful ⩓ Meal Times

A bright, striped table makes a kitchen cheery year-round.

Zigzag Floor »

A little white floor paint in a sharp design can transform a vinyl tile floor from ordinary to extraordinary. To create a design like this, adapt the technique used to paint a chevron design on end tables on page 86.

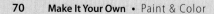

($)

Accent block

An accent block offers a fresh splash of color to a room and can function as a giant frame around any artwork you hang in its center.

Materials
- primer (if needed)
- latex paint, 1 quart

Tools
- carpenter's level
- pencil
- painter's masking tape, 1 inch or wider
- drop cloth
- ladder or step stool (if needed)
- paint tray
- roller, 9 inch or mini
- damp rag

Style Note

For a subtle effect, select a paint color that is close to the existing wall color but change the sheen—like a light blue glossy accent on a slightly darker blue matte wall. For a stronger effect, use a vividly contrasting color, or paint one rectangle inside another, using bright colors for both.

Steps

1. Draw the shape
With a carpenter's level and a pencil, establish the horizontal and vertical lines of the accent area's perimeter. Keep pencil lines light.

2. Tape
Just outside the pencil lines, outline the accent area with the painter's masking tape. It's fine to extend the tape past the corners. Press the tape tightly to the wall along the edges facing the accent area.

3. Prime
Position the drop cloth. If you are using primer, pour it into the tray. (See page 28 for when to prime.) With the roller, apply the primer from the tape toward the center of the accent block; avoid pushing the paint against the tape edge.

4. Paint
Pour the latex paint into a clean paint tray and apply the paint with the roller, using the same procedure of rolling the paint toward the center. Remove the tape promptly and wipe off any smears with the damp rag. Let dry.

5. Touch up and complete
If the paint looks thin or blotchy when dry, re-tape and add a second coat of paint. Remove the tape carefully.

First-Timer Tips

» The accent block doesn't have to be rectangular, but it should be large enough so as not to look like a picture frame, and yet not so large that it looks as though you simply forgot to finish painting the wall.

» Even when you press down firmly on the tape, paint still sometimes gets underneath it, especially on walls that have a distinct texture. To prevent this from happening, try this trick: After taping but before painting the accent block, brush a little of the main wall color along the accent side of the tape and let it dry. The paint will seep into any gaps and plug them, leaving no room for the accent color to sneak in there.

($)

Striped accent wall

Bedrooms are great places to try daring or colorful designs because only you will see them. If you're feeling brave, why not stripe an accent wall? Stripes are as versatile as they are playful. The effect is completely dependent on the colors you use.

Materials
- four colors of latex paint, 1 quart each

Tools
- ladder or step stool
- microfiber dust cloth
- rubber gloves, bucket, and sponge
- household cleaner, or deglosser if existing paint has a gloss finish
- painter's masking tape, 1 inch or wider
- tape measure
- pencil
- carpenter's level
- drop cloths
- synthetic-bristle brush, 1 inch to 1½ inch
- paint tray
- mini roller
- damp cloth
- artist's brush

Steps

1. Prep
Wipe the wall and the top of the baseboard with the dust cloth. If the wall is dirty, put on the gloves and wash the wall with the cleaner or deglosser. If you need to patch or prime, or want to repaint other surfaces first, follow the instructions on page 46. Apply painter's masking tape to the adjacent walls and the baseboard and ceiling along the wall to be striped. Press down firmly on the tape edges that face the accent wall.

2. Mark the verticals
Decide how wide you want each stripe to be. For stripes of equal width, measure the width of the wall with the tape measure and find an increment that divides into it evenly. Or plan to paint most of the wall with equally wide stripes in three colors, and use the fourth color for corner bands of a different width (as pictured). About mid-height on the wall, use the pencil and tape measure to mark the width of each stripe. From each mark, lightly trace with the pencil against the edge of the carpenter's level to create vertical lines the full height of the wall. Decide the order of color for the stripes, and label them on short pieces of painter's masking tape.

3. Paint the first stripes
Position the drop cloths. Paint the lightest-color stripes one at a time, using the synthetic-bristle brush to apply 2-inch-wide bands at the top and bottom of the wall. Then pour some paint into the tray and switch to the roller to fill in the middle. Paint a little over the lines. Let dry.

4. Paint the remaining colors
Redraw the lines you painted over, and apply painter's masking tape just beyond these lines on the newly painted sections so the colors will overlap slightly, preventing gaps. Apply the next-lightest color in the same way you did the first one. One edge of each stripe will have tape; the other will not. Remove the tape while the paint is damp so you can wipe off any smears with the damp cloth. Let dry. Mark, tape, and paint the remaining stripes in the same way. Touch up where needed with the artist's brush.

First-Timer Tip

Once you have applied tape to protect any stripes you just painted, brush a little of the previous color along the tape edges that face the unpainted stripes. This will prevent the new color from bleeding through.

Style Note

To create a calm look, use shades of a cool color (pictured here); to create a more vibrant look, paint colors that contrast more boldly (such as red and orange). For a kid's room, consider using a traditional or a pastel rainbow palette.

($) ($)

Dry-erase writing wall

Handwriting still has a place in this world—on your wall! Scrawl your favorite saying where everyone can see it. And change it as often as you like: This wall has a dry-erase finish.

Materials
- primer (type recommended for dry-erase finish)
- dry-erase (whiteboard) paint
- cardboard letter set
- dry-erase marker, fine tip or wider

Tools
- drop cloth
- ladder or step stool
- painter's masking tape, 1 inch or wider
- sandpaper or sanding sponge, 180 grit
- microfiber dust cloth
- synthetic-bristle brush, 2 inch or 3 inch
- paint tray
- foam roller (or the roller recommended on paint label), 9 inch
- carpenter's level
- chalkboard eraser or lint-free cloth

Steps

1. Prep
Position the drop cloth. To protect surrounding surfaces, apply painter's masking tape to the ceiling, baseboard, and flanking walls. Place the tape just beyond the edges of the wall you will paint. Press down firmly on the tape edges that face this wall.

2. Scuff or smooth
Assuming that the wall is smooth and already painted, scuff up the surface by sanding lightly with the sandpaper or sanding sponge. Remove the residue with the dust cloth. (If the wall has a textured surface, smooth it by following the instructions on page 59.)

3. Prime
Unless the dry-erase paint label says that priming is unnecessary, prime the wall following the priming instructions on page 46.

4. Apply the dry-erase finish
Using the brush, paint on the dry-erase finish following the painting instructions on page 59, unless the label suggests otherwise. Let dry. Apply additional coats if needed. Let dry.

5. Write
Wait for the paint to cure as long as the label recommends. Then, tape the cardboard letters to the wall to create a saying you like. If you need multiples of a letter, leave spaces where necessary, and come back to do those later. Use the carpenter's level to line up the bottom edges of all the letters in each line, and make sure the spacing between the letters is even. Then, trace around the cardboard letters with the dry-erase marker. Remove the cardboard and the tape. Tape up any of the letters that need to be used a second time in their places and trace them. You can erase your artwork with a chalkboard eraser or a lint-free cloth.

Maintenance Tip

To clean your new wall, use a nonabrasive cleaner. Let the surface dry completely before you start writing again.

LIFE IS SWEET

Style Notes

» Instead of painting a whole wall with dry-erase paint, make only a dry-erase accent block. Use the guidelines on page 72.

» Dry-erase paint comes in clear, white, and beige, and dry-erase markers come in all different colors, so have fun with the project!

$ $

Striped floor

Walls are not the only place to play with paint. Wooden floorboards are great candidates for painting. Color-striping your floor makes the room more cheerful and playful and can make the room seem bigger, too.

Materials
- primer, if recommended for the floor paint
- latex porch and floor paint, three or more colors

Tools
- sandpaper or sanding sponge, any grit between 100 and 220
- synthetic-bristle brush, 2 inch to 3 inch, depending on floorboard width
- rented orbital floor sander with 120-grit or 150-grit sanding discs
- vacuum
- rubber gloves, bucket, and sponge-type scrub pad
- knee pads (optional)
- household cleaner, or deglosser if the floor has a gloss finish
- painter's masking tape, 1 inch or wider
- paint tray
- mini roller
- artist's brush

Steps

1. Test the finish
Clean and lightly hand-sand a small, inconspicuous area. Wipe up the dust, then brush on a little paint. Let dry. If the paint wrinkles, bubbles, or lifts, the existing finish isn't suitable for painting. In that case, ask a professional floor finisher whether the floor can be stripped of its finish.

2. Wash the floor
If the test paint looked fine, put on the gloves and wash the floor with water and the cleaner or deglosser. Let dry.

3. Sand the floor
Scuff-sand the floor with the sander, just enough to make it evenly dull. Vacuum.

4. Prep and prime
Apply the painter's masking tape along the lower edge of the baseboard, and press the bottom edge down well. If the paint label recommends a primer, apply it now. Pour the primer into the paint tray and apply it with the roller, followed by a few smoothing strokes with the synthetic-bristle brush. Start in the corner farthest from the door and paint toward the door. Let dry.

5. Design the stripe pattern
Create a pattern for your stripes. Using the tape and the marker, label the floorboards for the colors you want.

6. Paint the first color
Start with the lightest color. Use the roller to apply the paint to the boards. Then use the brush, nearly dry, to even out the finish. Go over each area only once or twice, gently easing the brush up at the end of each pass. Let dry.

7. Paint the remaining colors and complete
Apply the painter's masking tape along both long edges of the boards you just painted. Then apply the next-darker color. Let that dry, then repeat the process of masking off the edges of the boards that already have their final color, and then applying the darker paint. Let dry. Remove the tape. With the artist's brush, touch up as needed.

First-Timer Tip

You can walk on the floor in stocking feet once the paint dries, but wait a couple of weeks, until the paint fully cures, before you put down a rug or replace furniture.

Style Notes

» For a coordinated look, use different shades of a single color (as pictured here). For a more playful look, use a few compatible colors in a random order.

» Preview your pattern by painting pieces of cardboard first and arranging them in the color order you plan to use on the floorboards.

($) ($) ($)

Stacked colorful crates

Create original and stylish shelving for books and collectibles by painting wine crates or other wooden packing containers, and stacking them any way you like.

Materials

(not including wooden boxes or crates)

- primer
- matte or semi-gloss latex paint, sample sizes

Tools

- sandpaper, 100 grit (if needed)
- microfiber dust cloth
- pencil
- ruler
- painter's masking tape, ½ inch or wider
- synthetic-bristle brush
- wood screws, a little less than twice as long as the thickness of the box sides
- drill with a bit slightly smaller in diameter than the screws
- screwdriver

Style Note

A colorful display cabinet looks even better when some of the accessories in it also feature the same colors—as pictured here.

Steps

1. Prep the boxes

Remove any dividers from the boxes. If there are rough spots, use the sandpaper to smooth the wood. Wipe off the residue with the dust cloth.

2. Design the layout

Stack the boxes and decide which ones should have color. On the back of each box, pencil in your color choice and the box's placement in the arrangement.

3. Tape

Apply tape to the front edges of each box you will paint. If the tape is wider than the wood, align the tape along the inside edges of the front surfaces.

4. Prime and paint

With the brush, apply primer to one box at a time in this order: the top surface, the back, the sides, and then the bottom. Repeat for all boxes. Let dry. Brush on the paint in the same fashion and let dry.

5. Attach the boxes

Restack the boxes. To attach adjoining boxes, drill holes in equidistant locations on the boxes. Use the screwdriver to set the first screw. Stop turning when the back of the screw head just touches the wood. Repeat with all the screws.

($)

Bedroom stencil

With the right stencil and some gold metallic paint, you can create a gorgeous floral design over your bed headboard—and wake up happy.

Materials
- floral or other stencil
- gold or other color metallic paint, sample size
- repositionable spray adhesive (optional)

Tools
- scrap paper, several sheets
- shallow container
- stencil brush
- drop cloth
- masking tape, any width
- damp rag

First-Timer Tip
There are all kinds of metallic paints, from translucent types to ones that develop a patina over time. But for this project, you need an opaque metallic paint that doesn't tarnish.

Steps

1. Design the layout
Take your stencil and place it on top of a sheet of scrap paper. Pour a little paint into the shallow container. Dab the tips of the stencil brush bristles into the paint, blotting the bristles to remove excess paint. Then dab straight down through the stencil to practice painting the design. Paint the edges of the cutout first, then the center. Repeat a few times on different sheets of paper, with the same element or a different one. Then arrange those pages to create a longer design that would look good on the wall. Use the damp rag to wipe any paint from the stencil, especially on the back.

2. Prep
Position the drop cloth. Tape the painted papers to the wall in the the order you selected. Stand back to see if you like the design. Reposition the sheets as needed.

3. Start the stencil
Take down one painted sheet and replace it with the stencil section that goes in its place. To attach it, spray the back of the stencil with repositionable spray adhesive, or use tape. Paint that part of the design. Clean the paint from the stencil.

4. Complete the design
Tape the next stencil section to the wall, replacing another painted sheet (that is *not* beside the area you just painted). Paint that part of the design. Continue skipping through the design. When the only areas left have wet paint nearby, pause until that paint dries, and then complete the project.

($)

Stencil-art roller shades

Blank white roller shades let in a lot of light, but they can also be a bit, well, blank. Add a little excitement to your shades by stenciling designs on them. It's easy and inexpensive—and your shades will be total originals.

Materials
(not including the fabric roller shades)

- printed image to copy (optional)
- stencil board or heavy card stock
- screen printing ink or fabric paint suitable for shade material

Tools

- photocopier
- glue stick
- cutting board, at least half the size of your image
- craft knife with extra blades
- drop cloth
- tape measure
- masking tape, any width, or repositionable spray adhesive
- stencil brush

Steps

1. Prep the image
Select an image from a clip-art book or Web site, or draw one yourself. With a photocopier, enlarge the image to the desired size, if necessary. For a larger image than your photocopier can handle, enlarge each half separately.

2. Create your stencil
With the glue stick, coat the back of the photocopy. Make sure to spread the glue onto all areas. Flip the image and adhere it to the stencil board or card stock. (If you enlarged halves of the image separately, glue each half to the board.) Let the glue dry. Then lay the stencil board on the cutting board. With the craft knife, carefully cut out the image. You may need to go over your cuts more than once to be able to lift out the image. Be sure to use sharp blades to avoid ragged edges; replace the blades as needed.

3. Position the stencil
Position one roller shade flat on the drop cloth with the room side facing up. Place the stencil on the shade. Use the tape measure to make sure the stencil is centered. Adhere the stencil (or multiple stencil sections) to the shade with masking tape or by spraying the back of the stencil with repositionable spray adhesive.

4. Paint
With the stencil brush, dab the printing ink or fabric paint through the stencil cutouts onto the shade. To keep the stencil tight against the shade (to prevent the ink or paint from seeping), press your fingers down on the stencil near the section you're painting. Let dry.

5. Set and hang
Remove the stencil and follow any paint label instructions for setting the color. Repeat on additional shades. Hang as you would any roller shade.

Style Note

To reverse the image for the second shade, as shown here, flip the stencil over. (Be sure that the ink or paint on the stencil board is completely dry before you flip the stencil!)

($) ($) ($)

Stenciled bath cabinet

Cotton swabs, medicine bottles, make-up—the bathroom cabinet isn't exactly the most exciting thing to look at. That is, until you make it over with painted-on stencils in an inside-out color scheme. Now, looking for a nail file becomes a whole lot more fun.

Materials

(not including materials for prepping, priming, and painting base coats)

- gloss or semi-gloss latex paint or enamel (two vividly contrasting colors)
- stencil with a dotted spiral or other all-over, repeating design
- repositionable spray adhesive

Tools

- scrap paper
- shallow container for paint
- stencil brush
- damp rag
- tape measure
- painter's masking tape, any width

Steps

1. Prep, prime, and paint

Follow the procedures on pages 62–63 to prep, prime, and paint the interior and exterior of the cabinet. Paint the interior with the color you'll use for the stenciled design on the front, and vice versa.

2. Create the design

Place a sheet of scrap paper under the stencil, and choose some elements from the stencil for the first part of your design. Pour a little paint into a shallow container, such as a discarded saucer or a large jar lid. Dab the tips of the bristles of the stencil brush into the paint, and blot them on a different piece of paper to remove excess paint, then paint that section of the stencil. Continue painting adjoining sections until you have enough pieces for the overall design.

3. Affix the design

With the tape measure, determine the height and width of the cabinet front. Mark the same dimensions on a flat surface, such as a tabletop or a section of the floor. Arrange the sample sheets there. Then use the painter's masking tape to affix them, sheet by sheet, to the cabinet front in the same arrangement.

4. Stencil the cabinet front

Remove one sample sheet, and tape up the stencil in its place, aligned to recreate that part of the design. Or, spray the back of the stencil with repositionable spray adhesive first and press the stencil to the cabinet. Paint that section of the stencil, using the technique you practiced in step 2. Always start at the edges of a cutout and paint toward the center. After you complete the section, remove the stencil and clean the back with the damp rag. Take down another sample sheet, not adjacent to where you just painted, reposition the stencil, and paint that section. Repeat until you complete the design. You may need to pause periodically to let the paint dry on adjoining sections.

5. Stencil the cabinet back

Stencil the back of the cabinet in the same way, using the contrasting paint color.

Style Note
Geometric patterns work well with this inside-out effect, but so do themed designs. For example, with a leaf stencil, you might want spring green leaves on the exterior and fall colors inside.

Maintenance Tip
If your cabinet is used a lot, brush a coat of matte acrylic over the completed stencil, especially on the exterior, after the paint fully dries.

($)

Chevron pattern

Chevrons, or inverted Vs, are a fun motif for all kinds of projects. You can send them marching across a tabletop or wall, or use rows of chevrons to join two end tables (as pictured here). Although the pattern looks complex, it is easier to create than it seems.

Materials
(not including tables)

- primer
- gloss latex paint (base color), 1 quart
- gloss latex paint (accent color), sample size

Tools

- drop cloth or newspaper
- sandpaper or sanding sponge, 180 grit
- microfiber dust cloth
- synthetic-bristle brush, 1 inch or 2 inch
- ruler
- scissors or craft knife
- painter's masking tape, 1 inch and 2 inch
- drafting triangle
- small chisel-tip artist's brush

Steps

1. Prep
Set the furniture you will paint on the drop cloth or newspaper. Remove any drawer handles or other add-ons, and lightly sand all the surfaces with the sandpaper. Remove residue by wiping with the dust cloth.

2. Prime and paint the base color
With the synthetic-bristle brush, apply one coat of primer to the entire piece. Let dry. Then paint the entire piece with your chosen base color. Let that dry, then apply a second coat. When the second coat is dry, apply a third coat to only the top surface. Let dry.

3. Design the first row
With the ruler and the scissors or craft knife, measure and then cut equal lengths of the 1-inch tape to establish the first row of zigzags. Test a few different dimensions of your own before settling on a design. Use the drafting triangle to keep the angles equal.

4. Complete the design
Directly beneath the first row of zigzags, create another zigzag pattern with the 2-inch tape (overlap the ends of the tape so no tabletop peeks out). Keep alternating the two sizes of tape until you cover the entire surface with zigzags.

5. Paint the pattern
Remove the strips of 1-inch tape. With the brush, apply the accent color to the exposed spaces. Let dry and then apply a second coat. Let dry.

6. Touch up and complete
Remove the remaining tape carefully. Do any necessary touch-ups with the artist's brush. Replace any drawer handles or add-ons.

Style Note

Painter's tape comes in various sizes. If you want narrower or wider stripes than those shown here, experiment with tape of different widths.

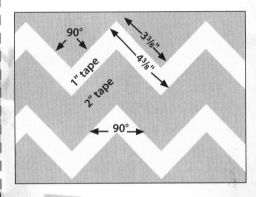

($)

Framed TV

Love your flat-screen TV? You'll love it even more in a frame. When it's off, it will look like sleek, geometrical art.

Materials
- molding for frame
- primer (unless molding is already primed)
- latex paint, 8 ounces

Tools
- tape measure
- miter box and saw
- corner clamps
- wood glue
- picture frame V-nails
- damp rag
- newspaper
- spacer blocks
- synthetic-bristle brush, 1 inch to 1½ inch
- picture hanger
- carpenter's level

Style Note
For the maximum trompe l'oeil effect, arrange other framed artwork nearby, and paint the TV frame to match some of the other frames.

▶ Steps

1. Determine the frame size

Decide how much of a border you want between the TV and the frame. Allowing for the width of the molding all around, determine the outside length and width of the frame.

2. Cut the miters

Using the miter box and saw, cut 45-degree angles pointed in opposite directions on the ends of each frame piece. From long tip to long tip, the measurements should match the lengths and widths you determined in step 1.

3. Assemble the frame

Work on one corner at a time. Tilt the frame pieces slightly as needed to align two edges, and then tighten the clamps at that corner. Fit the remaining corners in the same way. If you can't get a tight fit at a corner, clamp both frame pieces so the ends fit as well as possible, and then saw through the joint, shaving off a small amount from both sides (see below). Repeat this procedure, if needed, on the diagonally opposite corner.

Creating a tight fit

Clamp uneven frame pieces together.

Saw through the joint, shaving off a small amount from both sides to create a better fit.

4. Glue the frame

Once the whole frame is clamped together, loosen the clamps at one side of the corner that needed the least fussing. Remove that frame piece, spread glue on the end that fits into that corner as well as on the end of the mating frame piece that's still clamped. Put the frame piece back, retighten the clamps, and wait at least 15 minutes for the glue to set. Repeat this process at the other corners. When you get to the final piece, glue both ends at the same time.

5. Complete the frame

With the clamps still in place, flip the frame so that the back faces up. At each corner, hammer in two V-nails, one near the inside edge of the frame and the other toward the outside edge. The angle on each nail should lie over the joint, so the arms of the V point toward the inside edge of the frame. After you nail all the corners, remove the clamps and wipe off any excess glue with the damp rag.

6. Prime and paint

On newspaper, set the frame right side up on the spacer blocks. Brush the primer over all the visible frame edges. Smooth any drips as you go. Allow the primer to dry, then apply the paint in the same way. When it is dry, apply a second coat if needed.

7. Hang the frame

Attach the hanger parts to the back of the frame and to the wall. Hang the frame, adjusting it as necessary with the carpenter's level until it is level and the TV is centered.

First-Timer Tips

» Even when you use a miter box, it's tricky to cut a perfect 45-degree angle. If the store where you buy the molding can cut it for you, let them do it.

» Choose molding with a flat or grooved back. Crown molding, which is designed to fit at an angle between a wall and a ceiling, won't work.

5

Update furniture & accessories

Have an antique dresser from grandma? Mismatched candlesticks or picture frames? Most people discard old furniture and accessories when the paint fades or the fabric becomes worn. But you don't need to let go of those precious pieces from your past. Learn how to update them instead! With a little paint or fabric—and a lot of creativity—you can make them even better than new.

Mirror, Mirror ⩘

Mirrors aren't just for checking your hair—they are also accessories that reflect light. Frame a group of them in mismatched frames like these, and paint them a coordinated color, to give a lively boost to your bathroom.

Break with Tradition »

Paint is the best way to salvage furniture pieces you love. To transform an old breakfront cabinet like this one, all you need is sandpaper, primer, and a gorgeous hue or two.

Sunshine-y Dresser »

Yes, a dresser can be bright yellow, especially when juxtaposed with a rich blue wall as the backdrop. Dare to be bold with color—and update your furniture to create combinations that contrast and pop.

Chair makeover

Do you have an old, beaten-up chair that you still love? With some paint and a little fabric, you can turn a tired chair into a fresh, stylish eye-catcher.

Materials

(not including chair)

- primer, 1 quart
- matte latex paint, sample size
- fabric, ⅔ yard or as needed

Tools

- drop cloth or newspaper
- screwdriver
- sandpaper or sanding sponge, 180 grit
- microfiber dust cloth
- paint tray
- mini roller
- synthetic-bristle brush, 1 inch or 2 inch
- pencil or chalk
- scissors
- staple gun with ⅜-inch staples

First-Timer Tip

Make sure your chair is in good condition before you go through the trouble of making it over. Choose chairs with wooden frames, upholstered seats, no missing screws or loose legs, and interesting features or frame details.

▶ Steps

1. Prep

Place the chair on the drop cloth or newspaper. With the screwdriver, unscrew the seat from the chair frame. Set aside the seat and the screws. With the sandpaper or sanding sponge, lightly sand the frame. Wipe off the residue with the dust cloth.

2. Prime

Pour some primer into the tray. Use the mini paint roller to coat the frame with primer. Roll from the inside of the frame out toward the edges and from the top down. Then immediately follow with the brush to fill in the corners and remove drips. Brush in long, straight strokes to smooth the surface.

3. Paint

Apply a base coat of paint, following the same method used in step 2. Let the first coat dry and then apply a second coat. Let dry.

4. Re-cover the seat

Remove the old covering from the chair seat, or leave it on and apply the new covering over it. To cover the seat, put the seat face down on the fabric (also face down). If the fabric pattern includes stripes, make sure they align with the seat. Then, with the pencil or chalk, draw a line on the fabric 4 inches beyond the seat, or farther out if the seat is thick. With the scissors, cut along the line and remove the excess fabric. Wrap the seat fabric over

one edge of the seat, and secure it with two staples near the center of that edge. Pull the fabric snugly across to the opposite edge of the seat and repeat the stapling pattern. Repeat on the remaining two edges. Then, pulling the cloth tight, staple all around the perimeter, but stop 2 inches from each corner.

5. Staple the corners and complete

Pull the fabric tight over the seat at one corner and secure it with a staple to the back of the seat. Create neat tucks with the remaining fabric in that corner and staple them down (see illustration). Avoid stapling over the screw holes. Repeat for each corner. Once the paint on the frame is dry, reattach the seat to the frame with the screws you had set aside.

Style Notes

» Make a set out of mismatched chairs by unifying them with the same color and fabric.

» Use an accent color to paint the chair's smaller details. Choose something from the new seat-cover fabric to keep the color palette cohesive.

Staple the corners

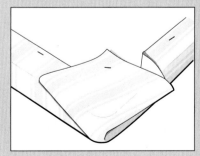

Pull the fabric tight at one corner and staple.

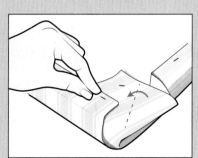

Create tucks with the remaining fabric.

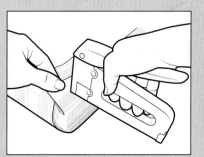

Staple the tucks.

Ⓢ

Glossy repainted candlesticks

Nearly everyone has a handful of mismatched candlesticks, but it's hard to display orphans, even if they're beautiful. Paint your solo candlesticks a single bold color to create a unified collection with dramatic punch.

Materials
(not including candlesticks)
- odorless paint thinner
- spray paint primer
- gloss spray paint

Tools
- nitrile gloves
- clean cloth
- drop cloth or newspaper
- protective goggles

Style Note
For a more dynamic look, use a fine artist's brush and a different color paint to accent a few details on each candlestick. For a subtler look, choose paint for the main color that has an eggshell finish instead of a gloss finish.

Steps

1. Clean
Put on the nitrile gloves. In a well-ventilated place, moisten the cloth with paint thinner and wipe each candlestick to remove all wax residue.

2. Prime
Apply the primer outdoors on a calm day, or in a well-ventilated place indoors where the paint fumes and any overspray won't cause a problem. Place one candlestick on the drop cloth or newspaper. Wearing the goggles and gloves, apply a light misting of primer, holding the spray can 12 to 14 inches from the candlestick. To prevent drips, keep the spray can at the same distance as you cover the candlestick evenly with paint. Let dry. Repeat for the other candlesticks. Between uses, wipe or clean the spray can nozzle as the label recommends.

3. Paint
Again working on one candlestick at a time, spray on two light coats of the glossy paint, allowing the paint to dry for the recommended time between coats. Keep the spray can at the same distance from the candlesticks as described above. Evenly cover the candlesticks, including the top rims. Let dry.

$ $

Colorfully framed photos

Create a unique photo display by painting mismatched picture frames with a carefully orchestrated palette. Voila!—an artful display suitable for any room in the house.

Materials
(not including wooden picture frames)

- black-and-white photographs
- five colors of latex paint, sample sizes
- precut mats, if needed

Tools

- sandpaper or sanding sponge, 180 grit
- microfiber dust cloth
- drop cloth or newspaper
- scraps of wood (to support frames while paint dries)
- synthetic-bristle brush, 1 inch or 1½ inch
- hammer
- picture hangers or nails

Style Note
For a sleeker look, paint all the frames the same color as the wall. Use only black-and-white photographs and see how they pop!

Steps

1. Design the layout
Arrange the frames and select which color to use for each.

2. Prep
Remove the mat and glass from each frame. Lightly sand any sheen off the wood with the sandpaper or sanding sponge. Remove any residue with the dust cloth.

3. Paint
Spread the drop cloth or newspaper, and arrange the wood scraps to support the frames. With the synthetic-bristle brush, paint the frames different colors.

4. Mat
When the frames are dry, buy precut mats for them, all in the same color. If you have a frame that a precut mat won't fit, choose a photograph that doesn't need a mat for that frame.

5. Mount
Assemble the mats and photographs in the frames. With the hammer, tap the picture hangers or nails into the wall and then hang the framed pictures.

$ $

Refinished dresser

Do you have a wooden dresser that looks a bit antiquated? With a little sanding and painting, turn it into a dramatic accent piece for your bedroom or hall.

Materials

(not including dresser)

- wood filler
- primer
- matte latex enamel (base color), 1 quart
- matte or glossy latex paint (accent color), sample size
- new wooden drawer pulls (optional)
- pads for dresser feet (optional)

Tools

- drop cloth or newspaper
- pencil
- screwdriver
- putty knife, 1 inch
- sandpaper or sanding sponge, 100 grit and 180 grit
- microfiber dust cloth
- paint tray
- mini roller
- synthetic-bristle brush, 1 inch or 1½ inch
- painter's masking tape, ½ inch and 1 inch
- artist's brush, preferably ¼ inch

▶ Steps

1. Take it apart

Place the dresser on the drop cloth or newspaper. Remove the drawers. Use the pencil to number each one on the back to identify where it fits. With the screwdriver, remove the drawer pulls and any wheeled feet, and set them aside. Remove any ornate parts that aren't essential and come off easily (such as the top trim in the "before" photograph).

2. Smooth out the surfaces

With wood filler and the putty knife, fill in any cracks and gaps, and the holes from any removed parts. Also smooth over any remaining fancy details that you want to conceal to create a more polished look. Once the filler is dry, sand the patches with the 100-grit sandpaper. Then scuff-sand all the surfaces with 180-grit. Wipe the surfaces with the dust cloth.

3. Prime and paint

Pour the primer into the paint tray. With the roller, prime all the visible surfaces on the dresser drawers and the case itself. Include the outside edges of the drawer fronts and the inside edges of the case where the drawers fit. As you prime each area, immediately follow up with the synthetic-bristle brush to remove any excess drips of paint. Brush with long strokes in the direction of the wood grain. If you are painting new drawer pulls (or want to repaint the old ones), prime them now. Rinse the tools and let the primer dry. Then use the same procedure to paint the drawers the base color. When the paint is dry, add a second coat. Let dry.

4. Create the detailing

Apply the 1-inch painter's masking tape along the front perimeter of the drawers where you want a stripe parallel with the edges. Apply the ½-inch tape just inside that, and then another round of 1-inch tape inside that, making three lines of tape with their edges abutting. Remove the ½-inch tape, leaving a tidy gap ½ inch wide. In a similar way, create ½-inch gaps for other design details, such as the jogs around some of the drawer pulls on the dresser in the photograph. When the pattern is complete, press down all the tape edges that face the ½-inch gaps. Use the brush to apply the accent paint onto the gaps and on the drawer pulls, too, if you have primed them. When the paint is dry, add a second coat. Let dry. Carefully remove the remaining tape.

5. Add the final details

Place the drawers back into the dresser. With the artist's brush, fill in any gaps in the design. Install the drawer pulls and any wheeled feet, or replace the wheels with pads that protect the floor.

Style Notes

» For a bolder look, keep the dresser color neutral but have fun with the accent color, like a dark green dresser with a bright yellow accent stripe. For a more subtle look, make the stripe the same color as the dresser, but in a different finish.

» If your dresser has a natural wood finish that you'd like to maintain, paint only the drawer fronts. For lighter wood, use white or black on the drawer fronts; for reddish wood, use dark green; for tan wood, use blue-violet.

$ $

Mirror-top side table

With some liquid silver and glass, you can take a dated, two-level side table from dingy to sleek and modern.

Materials

(not including side table)

- primer
- light-colored satin latex paint, sample size
- liquid silver leaf
- two pieces of mirrored glass, 3/16 inch thick, custom-cut at a glass store

Tools

- sandpaper or sanding sponge, 180 grit
- microfiber dust cloth
- drop cloth or newspaper
- synthetic-bristle brush, 1½ inch or 2 inch
- artist's brush

First-Timer Tip

When you measure the flat surfaces to order mirrors, take note of any special features of your furniture. (The side table pictured here, for example, has tapered legs, so the corners of the lower piece of glass had to be sanded off.)

Steps

1. Prep

These instructions assume that you have a two-tier table, but you can easily adapt them to accommodate any table with a flat surface. Lightly sand all surfaces of the table. Avoid rounding over the edges of flutes or other details that you will later paint with liquid silver. With the dust cloth, wipe away the residue.

2. Prime and paint

Set the table on the drop cloth or newspaper. With the synthetic-bristle brush, apply the primer over one surface at a time, working from the inside out and the top down. Coat all the surfaces, including the bottom of the tabletop, because it will be reflected in the lower mirror. Let dry. Apply the satin latex paint. Let dry, and then add a second coat.

3. Add the gilding

With the artist's brush, apply the liquid silver leaf on details you want to accent, such as the feet, various grooves, and the top edge (as pictured below).

4. Position the mirrors

Position the mirrors on the top of the table and on the lower shelf, but do not glue them down. (You'll be able to clean up spills more easily if the glass is removable.)

$

Multicolor filing cabinet

Transform your ho-hum filing cabinet in just a few hours with a little elbow grease and some fun bright paint.

Materials

(not including filing cabinet)

- primer that deactivates rust (if filing cabinet shows rust)
- primer for slick surfaces (this is the main primer)
- latex paint (two bright colors for the drawers, and a third color for the cabinet case if you want to paint it)

Tools

- drop cloth or newspaper
- screwdriver
- sandpaper or sanding sponge, 180 grit
- microfiber dust cloth
- synthetic-bristle brush, 1½ inch

Style Note

If you want a look that's a little more ornate, consider stenciling a geometric pattern on the front of the drawers. Choose a stencil with an all-over design, such as puzzle pieces, a trellis, or an array of polka dots. Use the color that's on contrasting drawers, or introduce a third color.

Steps

1. Prep

Empty the drawers, and remove them from the cabinet case. Set the drawers, front side up, on the drop cloth or newspaper. Using the screwdriver, detach the handles.

2. Scuff

Lightly sand the drawer fronts as well as their surrounding edges. Sand just enough to scuff up the surface. (If you want to paint the cabinet case itself, scuff up its exterior as well.) Wipe away the residue with the dust cloth.

3. Treat any rust

If you find rust, spot-prime it with a specialty primer that deactivates rust and prepares it for the main primer. Let dry.

4. Prime

With the brush, apply the main primer on the surfaces you sanded in step 2. Brush away any drips.

5. Paint

Brush on the latex paint. Paint every other drawer one color, then clean the brush and paint the remaining drawers with the other color. (Switch to a third color for the cabinet itself if you are painting it.) Let dry, then reattach the handles. Slide the drawers back into the cabinet.

Reborn vintage desk

With a little paint, some gold leaf, and a simple glass top, turn a run-down desk into a trendy, bold workstation.

Materials

(not including desk)

- wood filler
- primer, 1 quart
- brightly colored latex paint or latex enamel, gloss or semigloss, 1 quart
- gold paint marker
- liquid gold leaf
- custom-cut glass top with clear spacers (optional)

Tools

- screwdriver
- putty knife
- sandpaper or sanding sponge, 100 and 180 grit
- microfiber dust cloth
- drop cloth
- paint tray
- mini roller
- synthetic-bristle brush, 1 inch or 1½ inch
- artist's brush

Steps

1. Take it apart

Remove the drawers. With the screwdriver, take off the drawer pulls from the desk and set them aside.

2. Smooth the surfaces

With the putty knife, press wood filler into any large gashes and smooth the surface. Once the filler has dried, sand the patches with the 100-grit sandpaper. Then scuff up any parts of the desk and drawers that will be visible later with the 180-grit sandpaper. Wipe all the surfaces with the dust cloth.

3. Prime and paint

Position the drop cloth. Pour some primer into the tray. Working on one section at a time, use the roller to apply one coat of primer to the surfaces you sanded in step 2. Immediately after you prime each section, use the synthetic-bristle brush to remove any drips. Let dry. Then use the same procedure to apply two coats of latex paint. Let paint dry after each coat.

4. Add the gold detailing

With the gold paint marker, paint details such as the inner rims of the drawers (as pictured here).

5. Gild the drawer pulls and add glass

With the artist's brush, apply the liquid gold leaf to the drawer pulls. Let dry. Reattach the pulls and replace the drawers. Add the glass top with spacers, if desired.

Style Note

Create a mini art installation beneath the glass with photos, concert tickets, sports memorabilia, decorative paper, crushed flowers, or anything you like.

First -Timer Tip
Before you transform a hand-me-down desk, make sure it's worth the trouble. If the legs are so uneven that the piece wobbles, or if the drawers don't slide smoothly in their tracks, pass on this piece and continue your search for another one.

($) ($)

Refinished chandelier

Why buy a new lighting fixture when it's so easy to spiff up an old one? Just scan local thrift shops for a used chandelier, then give it a new paint job, bulbs, and shades.

Materials
(not including chandelier)

- spray paint
- energy-efficient flame-shaped bulbs
- candle sheaths
- mini shades from a lighting store (optional)

Tools

- small plastic bags
- painter's masking tape
- microfiber dust cloth
- drop cloth or flattened cardboard boxes
- protective goggles
- disposable gloves (latex or another material)

Steps

1. Prep
Take off all the removable parts from the chandelier, including the bulbs and sheaths. Using the small plastic bags and painter's masking tape, carefully cover all the exposed electrical parts, such as the bulb bases and the cord. Take the chandelier outside and hang it from a plant hook, clothesline, or other support. Clean all the surfaces with the dust cloth. If the chandelier is oily, clean it with water and a little detergent.

2. Paint
Apply the paint outdoors on a day that isn't windy. Hang the chandelier from a secure support, and spread the drop cloth or cardboard underneath it. Put on the protective goggles and disposable gloves. Apply a light coat of spray paint to the fixture. Hold the can 12 to 14 inches from the chandelier, and step around the chandelier to keep the distance and spray angle consistent. (If you simply pivot the can up and down or side to side, drips are likely to form.) Let the paint dry for at least 15 minutes, or as recommended on the can label, then spray with a second coat.

3. Buy new bulbs
Take the chandelier to a well-stocked hardware store, home center, or a shop that specializes in lightbulbs. Select new flame-shaped bulbs and candle sheaths that are compatible with your chandelier.

4. Dress it up (optional)
Add mini shades (as pictured here) to your chandelier.

Style Notes

» Decorate your chandelier with anything from crystal pendants to beads, shells, or feathers. Place any add-ons over the bars and beneath the bulbs, so nothing overheats.

» If you want to create the look of a brass chandelier, use a metallic paint. It won't look exactly like solid brass, but it will be close—especially when the lights are dimmed (and you are pouring the second round of wine!).

First-Timer Tip

If your chandelier has cracked wire insulation or rusted sockets, take it to a lighting repair shop and make sure it can be repaired before you repaint it.

6

Add style with wallcoverings

You can wake up any room by covering a few surfaces with a playful or bold pattern. With wallcoverings, anything goes—from botanical prints to stickers to traditional off-the-roll wallpaper. Your walls, stairway, bookcase—and even washing machine— can be transformed with your favorite colors and patterns. Just choose a design, follow our easy instructions, and change the whole look and feel of your room.

Spot Style »

Small splashes of wallpaper can transform even the simplest of cabinets into a piece with personality. For tips on how to wallpaper furniture like a pro, see the door panels on page 118 and the bookcase on page 126.

Oceanfront View ⩔

You may not be able to see the ocean from your window, but with a wallpapered accent wall, you can bring swimming sealife right into your bathroom.

Bold Bedroom Wall »

There's no need to wallpaper an entire bedroom to give it a new look. Choose a fresh, bright design and cover only one wall (see page 110). The results: less work, lower cost, and a chic look. Add contrasting pillows for extra punch.

$ $

Wallpaper accent wall

Wallpaper is making a comeback. Want to take part in the movement? There's no need to wallpaper an entire room the way people did years ago. Instead, choose a bright and bold pattern and use it on just one accent wall. You cut the cost, speed the work, and wind up with a room that sings.

First-Timer Tips

» Take along a sketch or photo of the wall and its dimensions when you shop for wallpaper. Once you find a pattern you like, ask a clerk at the store to help you calculate how much wallpaper to buy.

» If the wall already has wallpaper, you may be able to paper over it after you apply a coat of wallcovering primer with sizing. But if the old wallpaper is loose or peeling, you must strip the existing wallpaper and start from scratch.

Alternate Method

If you use unpasted wallcovering instead, simply ask for the correct adhesive at the wallcovering store—and for a pamphlet or a flier detailing the procedure.

Materials

- drywall mud or spackle (if the wall needs patching)
- acrylic wallcovering primer with sizing
- pre-pasted wallpaper

Tools

- drop cloths
- ladder or step stool
- rubber gloves, bucket, and sponge
- household cleaner, or deglosser if existing paint has a gloss finish
- putty knife (if wall needs patching)
- paint tray
- roller, 9 inch or mini
- synthetic-bristle brush, 1½ inch or 2 inch
- tape measure
- pencil
- carpenter's level
- scissors
- wallpaper water tray
- wallpaper brush and wallpaper sponge
- seam roller
- taping knife, 6 inch to 10 inch
- single-edge razor blade

continued on page 112

▶ Steps

1. Prep and prime

Spread the drop cloths. Wearing gloves, wash the wall with water and the cleaner or deglosser. Let dry. To patch any holes, apply the drywall mud or spackle with the putty knife. Let dry. Pour some primer with sizing into the paint tray and prime the wall; use the roller for the main expanse of the wall and the synthetic-bristle brush for the corners. Let dry.

2. Find the starting point

With the tape measure and the pencil, measure the wall's width and mark the midpoint. Then, using the wallpaper roll as a guide, mark wallpaper-width increments across the wall to the edges. If less than half the paper's width is left over at each corner, plan to center the first strip over the wall's midpoint (see the top illustration). Otherwise, plan to have the first two pieces flank the wall's midpoint (see the bottom illustration). For either case, use the pencil and the carpenter's level to draw a vertical line ¼ inch to the left of where the left edge of the first strip will be (so the pencil mark won't show in the seam).

3. Cut the paper

Measure the wall's height. On the floor, unroll a length of the paper. Choose what part of the pattern you want at the top of the wall. Allowing an extra 2 inches at the top and bottom, cut off the strip with the scissors. Unroll another length of wallpaper, line up the pattern with the first strip, and cut to length. Repeat for the remaining pieces.

4. Paste

Roll one strip so the pasted side faces out. Add water to the wallpaper water tray. Submerge the rolled strip in the water. Grab the paper's top edge and lift the sheet from the water as it unrolls. Place the strip right side down on the drop cloths. Loosely fold the top and bottom edges toward the center, so no sticky side faces out. Wait the recommended "booking" time (see page 34).

5. Apply

Unfold the top half of the paper and align it with 2 inches extra at the top, ¼ inch to the right of the guide line (from step 2). Working your way down, smooth the paper against the wall with your fingertips and the wallpaper brush. Brush from the center toward the sides. Prepare and position the remaining sheets in the same way, butting the edges tightly together. About 15 minutes after you apply each sheet, roll over the edges with the seam roller. Wipe the wallpaper with the damp wallpaper sponge.

6. Trim

To trim the top and bottom edges, place the taping knife over the wallpaper and press the tool's thin edge into the edge. Trace against the edge with the razor blade, neatly slicing off the 2-inch excess.

Find the starting point

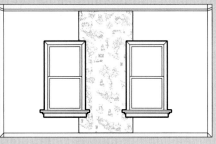

Center the first strip over the wall's midpoint.

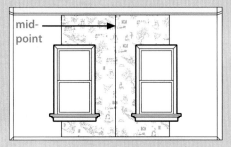

Place the first two pieces so they flank the wall's midpoint.

$ $ $

Botanical wall

Botanical prints make fantastic wallpaper and give rooms an old-world feel.

Materials

- botanical prints
- acrylic wallcovering primer with sizing
- clear, strippable wallcovering adhesive, labeled for all wallcovering types

Tools

- single-edge razor blades or craft knife
  with extra blades
- cutting board
- drafting triangle
- ruler
- drop cloths
- ladder or step stool
- rubber gloves, bucket, and sponge
- household cleaner, or deglosser
  if existing paint has a gloss finish
- tape measure
- pencil
- carpenter's level
- wallpaper sponge and wallpaper
  brush
- paint tray
- roller, 9 inch or mini
- synthetic-bristle brush, 2 inch or
  2½ inch
- taping knife, 6 inch to 10 inch

Steps

1. Design the wallpaper

Find botanical prints in old books or calendars. Cut out the pages with the razor. On the cutting board, square up the edges of the prints with the drafting triangle, ruler, and razor.

2. Prep and prime

Position the drop cloths on the floor. Wearing the gloves, wash the wall with water and the cleaner or deglosser. Let dry. Pour some primer with sizing into the paint tray and prime the wall; use the roller for the main expanse of the wall and the synthetic-bristle brush for the corners. Let dry. With a damp sponge, wipe off any of the primer that gets onto adjoining surfaces.

3. Find the starting point

Measure the width of the wall and mark the midpoint. Assuming that all the prints are the same size, measure their width and mark that increment across the wall, starting in the center of the wall. If less than half the print width is left over at each corner, plan to center the first print over the wall's midpoint (see the top illustration on page 115). Otherwise, plan to have the first two pieces flank the wall's midpoint (see the bottom illustration on page 115). For either case, use the pencil and carpenter's level to draw a

continued on next page

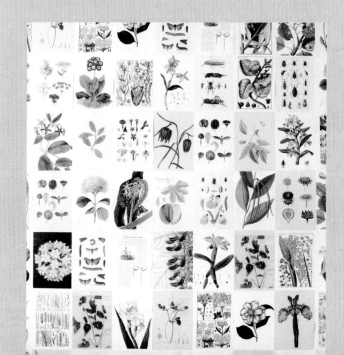

vertical line ¼ inch to the left of where the left edge of the first print will be (so the pencil line won't show when the print is positioned). If the print widths differ, design a layout first by holding the prints to the wall with pushpins. If they are all the same, keep the rows even. Avoid having any narrow strips of partial posters at the corners.

4. Install the first row

With the brush or roller, spread a thin, even layer of the wallcovering adhesive where you'll place the first print, at the top of the wall and ¼ inch to the right of the guide line (from step 3). Press down the top edge of the print, and then work your way down, using your fingers and the wallpaper brush to smooth out any air bubbles. Go over the whole sheet again, stroking with the brush from the center out. Wipe off excess adhesive with a damp wallpaper sponge. Apply the next sheets in the same way until you reach the adjoining walls.

5. Trim the corners

When you're approaching each corner, measure the distance between the already positioned print and the corner, and add ½ inch. Cut the edge print to that dimension with the razor on the cutting board. Glue the cut print to the wall as usual, but let the corner edge wrap loosely onto the next wall. Press the taping knife into the corner, and fold back the entire far edge of the print, creasing it against the blade. Then pull the print out slightly from the corner, and cut along the crease with a sharp razor blade. Press the cut edge back into place. Wipe off any excess adhesive with a damp wallpaper sponge.

6. Complete the wall

Install the remaining rows of prints in the same way. Every couple of rows, stop to make sure the prints are still aligned. To trim the bottom edge of the final row of prints, you can simply use the taping knife as a straightedge and trim the sheets in place with the razor.

Find the starting point

Center the first strip over the wall's midpoint.

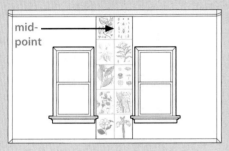

Place the first two pieces so they flank the wall's midpoint.

Ⓢ

Map-covered wall

Maps make great wallpaper, doubling as geography study guides or simply travel inspiration.

Materials

- maps
- acrylic wallcovering primer with sizing
- clear, strippable wallcovering adhesive labeled for all wallcovering types

Tools

- ladder or step stool
- pushpins
- carpenter's level
- pencil
- drop cloths
- painter's masking tape, 1 inch or wider
- rubber gloves, bucket, and sponge
- household cleaner, or deglosser if existing paint has a gloss finish
- paint tray
- roller, 9 inch or mini
- synthetic-bristle brush, 2 inch or 2½ inch
- wallpaper brush
- tape measure
- scissors
- taping knife, 6 inch to 10 inch
- single-edge razor blade
- wallpaper sponge

Steps

1. Design the wall

Arrange the maps on the wall, using pushpins to hold them in place temporarily and the carpenter's level to make sure they are level. Maps that you want to leave whole should go toward the middle. If you find that there is a narrow strip of map along one side wall, shift the whole row and plan to trim both end maps so they are approximately the same width. As you take down the maps, mark their locations on the back with the pencil.

2. Prep

Position the drop cloths. Use the painter's masking tape to mask off the baseboard. Wearing gloves, wash the wall with water and the cleaner or deglosser. Let dry. Pour some primer with sizing into the tray and apply it to the wall, using the roller for the main area and the synthetic-bristle brush for the corners. Let dry.

3. Install the first row

With the brush or the roller, spread a thin, even layer of wallcovering adhesive at the center of the top row. Line up the pushpin marks in the map and the wall, and press the top edge of the first map in place. Then, working from top to bottom, press the rest of the map to the wall, using your fingers and the wallpaper brush to smooth out bubbles and folds. With a barely damp wallpaper sponge, blot any excess adhesive. Then coat the next area with the adhesive and apply the next map in the same way.

4. Trim the corners

When you get near each corner, measure the distance to the corner and add ½ inch. With the scissors, cut the map to that dimension. Glue the map to the wall in the usual way, but let the corner edge wrap loosely onto the adjacent wall. With the taping knife, press the map into the corner and then fold back the entire edge, creasing it against the knife blade. Pull the map edge a little out from the corner, and cut along the crease with the razor blade. Then press the cut edge back into place. Wipe off any excess adhesive with the moistened sponge.

5. Complete the wall

Install the additional rows in the same way. To trim the maps along the bottom edge, press the sheets into the ridge between the wall and the baseboard and cut them with the razor blade.

First-Timer Tip

To simplify this project, stop adding rows of maps when you're so low that full sheets no longer fit (as pictured here).

Style Note

The background color of the maps is the most important thing to consider when using them as wallpaper. Make sure the ones you choose go well together.

($) ($) ($)

Wallpapered door panels

Some of the most attractive wallpaper patterns are too busy for an entire room, but perfect for transforming a small area, such as a door. Liven up your doors with this simple yet dramatic idea.

Materials

- 1 double roll of wallpaper, pre-pasted or unpasted
- acrylic wallcovering primer with sizing
- clear strippable wallcovering adhesive, labeled for all wallcovering types (if wallpaper is unpasted)

Tools

- ruler
- drafting triangle
- pencil
- sticky notes (Post-Its)
- scissors
- household cleaner, or deglosser if existing paint has a gloss finish
- rubber gloves, bucket, and sponge
- synthetic-bristle brush or sponge brush, 2 inch
- wallpaper smoothing tool
- wallpaper sponge

▶ Steps

1. Measure and cut

With the ruler, measure the door panels. Then, using the ruler, drafting triangle, and pencil, lightly outline the shapes on the face of the wallpaper. On the sticky notes, mark the placement of the shapes and which end of each shape will face the top of the door. With the scissors, cut the wallpaper exactly to fit.

2. Prep and prime

Wearing gloves, wash the door with water and the cleaner or deglosser. Let dry. With the brush, apply a thin, even coat of wallcovering primer with sizing to each door panel. (This helps the wallpaper stick to gloss paint, which is commonly used on doors. The primer with sizing also makes the wallpaper easier to remove later.) Wipe away any drips with the damp sponge. Let dry.

3. Apply the wallpaper

If the wallpaper is unpasted, use the clean brush to apply a thin, even coat of the adhesive onto one door panel. If you're using pre-pasted paper, brush water (instead of adhesive) onto the back of the paper and wait the recommended "booking" time (see page 34). In either case, press the wallpaper onto the door panel. If you see that the paper isn't aligned properly, slide it gently into position. Smooth the paper with your fingers as you go. Then go over the sheet with the smoothing tool, working from the center toward the edges. Sponge off any excess adhesive with the wallpaper sponge. Repeat for the other door panels.

4. Press the edges and complete

After applying wallpaper to each panel, wait about 15 minutes and then press around the edges of the wallpaper with your fingers one more time. Wipe the surface again with the wallpaper sponge.

Save Money

A typical minimum order of wallpaper is a double roll of 11 yards or more, which can be pricey. For a project like this, search online for "wallpaper by the yard" to find companies that sell shorter lengths. The price per yard might be twice as high, but the overall cost will be lower.

Style Note

To get a symmetrical look, have matching images on each door panel. To do this, select a wallpaper pattern that repeats often enough so that you won't waste a lot of paper between the design sections you want.

First-Timer Tip

Pay attention to how the pattern repeats. If you want the design to appear as if it runs uninterrupted from the bottom of the door to the top, leave intervals for the door rails between your cutting lines.

Alternate Method

Instead of pasting the wallpaper to the door panels, you can use permanent double-face tape. The process is neater, but the tape will be harder to remove than the wallpaper paste if you change your mind later on.

$ $ $

Wallpapered stairs

Most people think that wallpaper is just for walls. But you can wallpaper almost anything—including a staircase that needs sprucing up.

Materials

- 1 roll (or 1 double roll) of wallpaper, pre-pasted or unpasted
- acrylic wallcovering primer with sizing
- clear strippable wallcovering adhesive, labeled for all wallcovering types (if wallpaper is unpasted)
- matte or gloss clear acrylic, 1 quart

Tools

- ruler
- drafting triangle
- pencil
- sticky notes (Post-Its)
- scissors
- household cleaner, or deglosser if existing paint has a gloss finish
- rubber gloves, bucket, and sponge
- synthetic-bristle brush or sponge brush, 2 inch
- wallpaper sponge and wallpaper brush
- wallpaper smoothing tool
- painter's masking tape, 1 inch or wider
- newspaper (optional)

▶ Steps

1. Measure and cut

With the ruler, measure each stair riser separately, as there may be discrepancies in height or length. Using the ruler, drafting triangle, and pencil, lightly outline the rectangles you will need on the face of the wallpaper. Use the sticky notes to indicate the order of the risers, and which edge faces up. Cut the wallpaper exactly to fit each riser.

2. Prep

Wearing gloves, wash the steps with water and the cleaner or deglosser. Let dry. With the wallpaper brush, apply a thin, even coat of wallcovering primer with sizing to each riser. (This helps the wallpaper stick to the slick surfaces common on stair risers, such as lacquer and gloss paint, and it makes the wallpaper easier to remove later.) Wipe away any drips with the wallpaper sponge. Let dry.

3. Apply the wallpaper

If you're using unpasted wallpaper, brush a thin coat of adhesive on one stair riser. Use enough to cover the riser completely but not so much that it drips. If you're using pre-pasted paper, brush water onto the back of the paper, and wait the recommended "booking" time (see page 34). In either case, press the wallpaper onto the first riser, starting at one corner and working your way across. If you see that the paper isn't aligned properly, slide it gently into position. Smooth the paper with your fingers as you go. Then go over the sheet with the smoothing tool, working from the center toward the edges. Sponge off any excess adhesive with the wallpaper sponge. Repeat for the other risers.

4. Press the edges and complete

About 15 minutes after you've applied each sheet of wallpaper, press around the edges with your fingers one more time. Wipe off the surface again with the wallpaper sponge.

5. Add the glaze

After the wallpaper adhesive is completely dry, you can add a glaze of clear acrylic to protect the wallpaper and make scuffs easier to wipe off. First, apply the painter's masking tape just outside the edges of each riser to protect the adjoining surfaces from the glaze. For extra protection, position sheets of newspaper on the stair treads. Using the synthetic-bristle brush or sponge brush, apply the clear acrylic over the wallpaper; it will look milky at first but will become transparent when it's dry.

Alternate Method

If you want to avoid using water or messy adhesive, you can use permanent double-faced tape. The downside is that the tape is harder to remove than the wallpaper paste if you change your mind later.

First-Timer Tips

» A staircase is usually wider than a wallpaper roll, so choose a pattern that looks good sideways. This way, you'll need only one strip per stair. Also, some designs will produce wildly varying effects on each stair, so choose your wallpaper with this in mind.

» Unpasted wallpaper is recommended over pre-pasted wallpaper for this project because it calls for a gel adhesive rather than water to apply the paper to the surface. This is helpful if you don't want to drip water onto your stairs, which might damage the finish on the treads.

$ $ $

Coordinated desk and accessories

You can easily perk up your desk by topping it with wallpaper. And one double roll of wallpaper—usually the minimum you can buy—has plenty of paper left over to lift the spirits of all sorts of accessories, from pencil holders to wastebaskets. The result: a fun, coordinated look that's all your own.

Materials
(not including the desk or accessories)

- wallpaper, pre-pasted or unpasted
- custom-cut glass top with clear spacers
- clear spacers (for the glass)
- clear strippable wallcovering adhesive, labeled for all wallcovering types (if wallpaper is unpasted)

Tools

- tape measure
- ruler or yardstick
- pencil
- scissors
- transparent tape (for desk project)
- synthetic-bristle brush, 1 inch or 1½ inch
- wallpaper sponge

Steps

COVER A DESK

1. Measure the desk
With the tape measure, measure the length and width of the top of the desk. Give the measurements to a glass shop and order a custom-cut piece of glass with smoothed edges and clear spacers.

2. Cut the wallpaper and cover the desk
Decide whether to run the wallpaper horizontally (a single strip across the desk) or vertically (several shorter strips side by side). On the back of the wallpaper, use the pencil and ruler or yardstick to mark the lengths and widths you need to create a rectangle that matches the dimensions you measured in step 1. Cut along the lines.

3. Assemble
If you cut several pieces of wallpaper to cover the desk, tape them together on the back. Place the wallpaper right side up on the top of the desk and match the edges to the desk edges. Set the spacers on the wallpaper, then lower the glass into place.

Alternate Method
Instead of leaving the wallpaper loose and covering it with glass, glue the wallpaper to the desk. When the glue is dry, brush a coat or two of clear acrylic over the paper to protect it and create a surface that you can wipe clean.

Style Note
Leave some accessories unadorned so the wallpaper-covered ones stand out as accents. If you overdo the accents, they'll lose their punch.

continued on page 124

First-Timer Tip
If you are using pre-pasted wallpaper to cover the accessories, go back about 15 minutes later and press down any seams that appear loose.

COVER BOXES

1. Measure

Measure down from the top edge of one long side of the box across the bottom and up the opposite side, and add 2 inches. That is one dimension of the wallpaper sheet you need to cover the box. Find the other dimension by measuring down from the top edge of one short side, across the bottom and up the opposite end; again add 2 inches.

2. Cut the wallpaper

On the back of the paper, use the pencil and the ruler or yardstick to mark a rectangle to the adjusted dimensions you calculated found in step 1. Cut along the lines. Position the paper, right side down, and center the box on it. Check with the ruler to make sure that the paper overlaps by the same distance at each end and each side. With the pencil, trace around the bottom edge of the box. Set the box aside. Then use the ruler and the pencil to extend the box's length lines to the edges of the paper. Create flaps by cutting along these extension lines (see illustration).

3. Assemble

Dampen the wallpaper with the sponge if it's the pre-pasted type, or brush the wallcovering adhesive on the back of the unpasted wallpaper (or on the box). Center the box within the outline of the box bottom. Starting with one long edge, fold up the paper and smooth it against the side of the box. Fold the flaps you cut in step 2 onto each narrow end of the box. At the top corners, clip straight down with the scissors as far as the box (see illustration). Fold the extra inch of paper to the inside and glue it down. Cover the other long edge of the box in the same way. Finally, fold the remaining paper up and over the ends of the box.

4. Cover the lid

Treat the lid as a shallow box. Cover it using the same procedure described in steps 1, 2, and 3.

COVER A CYLINDER

1. Measure

With the ruler or tape measure, determine the height of the container you want to cover. (If it's a can, you might want to measure between the top and bottom lips, since those make tidy edging if left uncovered.) To determine the container's circumference, wrap the wallpaper around it and mark where the paper begins to overlap, or place the container on its side and roll it one full turn over the paper.

2. Cut the wallpaper

On the back of the wallpaper, use the pencil and the ruler or yardstick to mark a rectangle that's as wide as the height you found in step 1 and as long as the circumference plus 1 inch, to allow an overlap. Cut out the shape.

3. Assemble

Dampen the wallpaper if it's the pre-pasted type, or brush the wallcovering adhesive on the back of the unpasted wallpaper. Wrap the paper around the container. Press the seam down well. With a damp wallpaper sponge, wipe off any adhesive on the front of the paper. After 15 minutes, press down the seam again.

Cover a box

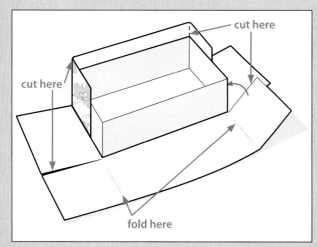

cut here

cut here

fold here

COVER A BINDER

1. Measure

Open the binder so both covers and the center rib are flat
against your work table. Measure the overall length and width,
and add 3 inches to each dimension. That's the length and width
you need for the wallpaper cover.

2. Cut the wallpaper

Place the wallpaper right side up. Decide which design elements
you want to include in your binder cover, and place the binder
over them. Check that all the key elements you want are covered
and that any straight lines in the pattern line up with the edges
of the binder. Measure out 3 inches in a couple of places from
each side of the binder and make short pencil marks. With the
ruler and pencil, draw through those marks to complete a
rectangle the size of the wallpaper cover. With the scissors, cut
along the lines.

3. Assemble

Dampen the wallpaper if it's the pre-pasted type, or brush the
adhesive on the back of the unpasted wallpaper. With the back
of the wallpaper facing up, center the outside face of the binder
on the paper. Slip your hand underneath and press the paper to
the center rib. Lift one cover at a time, and press the wallpaper
to its outside surface. There will still be an unattached band of
paper around the perimeter. Clip diagonally across it at each
corner, then fold the flaps to the inside and glue them down. Clip
as needed to fit the paper around the center rib. With a damp
wallpaper sponge, wipe off any adhesive on the front of the
paper. Let dry.

($)($)($)

Wallpapered bookcase

Books aren't boring and your bookcase shouldn't be, either. Turn a standard wood or inexpensive particleboard bookcase into a conversation piece by covering it with lively wallpaper.

Materials
(not including bookcase)

- primer for slick surfaces, 1 quart
- latex paint for front edges, 8 ounces
- two to four double rolls of unpasted wallpaper
- clear strippable wallcovering adhesive, labeled for all wallcovering types

Tools

- drop cloths and spacer blocks
- rubber gloves, bucket, and sponge
- household cleaner, or deglosser if existing paint has a gloss finish
- paint tray
- mini roller
- synthetic-bristle brush, 1 inch or 1½ inch
- tape measure
- pencil, yardstick, drafting triangle, and scissors
- paint pad
- wallpaper brush and wallpaper sponge
- craft knife with sharp blade

▶ Steps

1. Prep and prime

Remove all moveable shelves and shelf supports from the bookcase. Place the bookcase on one drop cloth and place the shelves on the spacer blocks on another drop cloth. Wearing gloves, wash the case and the shelves with water and the cleaner or deglosser. Wipe off all residue. Let dry. Pour some primer into the tray. Using the mini roller, apply the primer to the top side and the front edge of each shelf. Also roll primer onto the case, coating the inside, then the outside, and finally the front edges. Use the synthetic-bristle brush to get into the corners and to remove drips. When the shelves are dry, flip them and prime the other side. Let dry.

2. Paint the front edges

With the brush, apply the latex paint to the front edges of the bookcase and the front edges of the shelves. Brush away any drips. It's okay if some paint gets onto surfaces that you will cover with wallpaper. Let dry overnight.

3. Cut the wallpaper

With the tape measure, determine the wallpaper sizes you need for both sides of the shelves, the bookcase perimeter, and the back panel. Using the pencil, yardstick, and drafting triangle, outline the shapes you need on back of the wallpaper, and cut them out with the scissors.

4. Apply the wallpaper

If you're using unpasted wallpaper, brush a thin, even coat of the adhesive onto the back panel of the bookcase. If you're using pre-pasted paper, place each piece for the back panel upside down on the drop cloth or a covered table. Dampen the surface using the paint pad and water. Loosely fold each end of the wallpaper to the middle (so the water doesn't evaporate before the adhesive can absorb it). Wait the recommended "booking" time (see page 34). Then attach one sheet of wallpaper at a time to the back panel. Unfold only the top section at first. Line up the top edge, then work your way down, smoothing the paper with finger pressure and the wallpaper brush. Then go over the whole sheet with the brush, working from the center out, to remove air bubbles. Wipe with the damp wallpaper sponge. In the same way, wallpaper the rest of the bookcase interior, then its exterior, and finally the shelves. Let the adhesive dry.

5. Replace the shelves

With your fingers, locate the holes for the shelf supports by pressing on the wallpaper on the interior side surfaces. With the pencil tip, poke through the holes you want to use, and trim with the craft knife. Replace the shelf supports, then add the shelves.

Style Note

If the current finish on the bookcase is attractive, you can wallpaper only the interior, exterior, or shelves and let the existing finish show on the other surfaces.

Ⓢ

Decal-covered washing machine

If your laundry room needs a little brightening, make your washing machine a chic centerpiece with decorative vinyl decals. You can get them in all kinds of patterns—from trees to geometric designs.

Materials
- vinyl decals (the type with a transfer sheet)

Tools
- clean cloth
- detergent
- scissors
- painter's masking tape
- soft, dry sponge or a plastic credit card

Steps

1. Clean the surface
Wipe the front of the washing machine with a clean cloth moistened in warm water and detergent. Wipe away residue. Let dry.

2. Trim the decals
Decide roughly how you want the design to fit around the washer door. Decals usually come with each color of the design elements on a separate sheet. Use the scissors to cut the pieces apart. You don't need to worry about trimming the cutouts to the exact decal shapes, but do keep together any design elements that you want to use as they are currently aligned. Keep the decals sandwiched between the backing sheet and the transfer sheet during this step and the next.

3. Arrange the pieces
With the painter's masking tape, temporarily affix the cutouts to the washer. Rearrange them until you like the way the design appears. If you want to overlap some design elements, plan which decals you need to apply first to achieve the look you want. For example, if you have decals that show a flowering cherry tree, you would apply the trunk first, then the blossoms.

4. Attach the decals
Begin in a convenient spot, like one of the lower corners of the design. Remove the decal or decals that will be affixed in this area and decide which one to apply first. Place the decal with its design side down on a flat, hard surface. Rub the back with your hand or the plastic card to shift the decal weight to the transfer sheet. Peel away the backing along its top edge, leaving the decals still attached to the transfer sheet. Affix the peeled-back strip to the washer in the appropriate spot. Then peel off the rest of the backing by pulling it downward as you smooth the outside of the transfer sheet with your other hand. Go over the surface again with the dry sponge or the plastic card to smooth out any bubbles or wrinkles. Finally, peel off the transfer sheet.

5. Complete the design
Repeat step 4 for the other parts of the design.

First-Timer Tip
If the design includes a lot of small parts, it's not necessary to decide where every detail will go. Plan the main elements, and then arrange the smaller elements spontaneously as you install them.

($)

Decal headboard

If you love the look of a decorative headboard, but prefer to prop pillows right up against the wall while sitting up in bed, create a faux headboard with a decal. You can do this whether you own your home or rent an apartment because the decal peels off the wall when it's time to move.

Materials
- vinyl headboard decal

Tools
- microfiber dust cloth
- rubber gloves, bucket, and wallpaper sponge
- household cleaner
- scissors
- painter's masking tape
- carpenter's level
- pencil
- soft, dry sponge or a credit card

Style Note
Headboard decal styles range from Victorian ornate—think iron beds with lots of little metal curlicues—to simple modern designs. If you want a marriage of both, look for a fresh take on a classic shape, like the design in the photo.

Steps

1. Clean the wall
Wipe the wall with the dust cloth. If it picks up oily residue, put on the gloves and wash the wall with warm water and a little household cleaner. Wipe away residue with the wall-paper sponge, and let dry.

2. Trim the decal
With the scissors, cut the decal into three sections (unless it is already in sections): one top piece and two side pieces. Keep the sections sandwiched between the backing sheet and the transfer sheet during this step.

3. Arrange the pieces
With the painter's masking tape, temporarily affix the decal sections to the wall. With the carpenter's level, make sure the side sections are perfectly vertical and their top edges are aligned horizontally. With the pencil, lightly mark the locations of all the sections so you can arrange them in the same positions later.

4. Install the top piece
Remove the top decal (but leave the decals for the side posts in place). Place the decal with its design side down on a flat, hard surface. Rub the back with your hand or the plastic card to shift the decal weight to the transfer sheet. Peel away the backing along the top. Align the decal with the pencil marks you made in step 3 and affix the peeled-back area to the wall in the appro-priate spot. Then peel off the rest of the backing by pulling it downward as you smooth the outside of the transfer sheet with your other hand. Go over the surface again with the dry sponge or plastic card to smooth out any bubbles or wrinkles. Finally, peel off the transfer sheet.

5. Complete the design
Repeat step 4 for the side pieces.

First-Timer Tip

If you want to paint the wall before you apply the decal, plan ahead. Manufacturers often recommend waiting two weeks to one month before applying a decal to fresh paint. If you do repaint, use semi-gloss latex paint; decals grip best to that type of paint.

$ $ $

Artful framed wallpaper

Wallpaper can be a work of art in itself. Select and frame pages from a wall-paper sample book, using different patterns but a unified theme.

Materials
- wallpaper sample book (ask a wall-covering store for a free book of discontinued styles)
- 20 white picture frames with mats, 8 inch by 10 inch

Tools
- utility knife and extra blades
- cutting board
- pencil
- ruler
- microfiber dust cloth
- hammer
- picture hangers or nails
- tape measure
- carpenter's level

Steps

1. Choose the art
Select pages in the wallpaper book that you would like to frame. With the utility knife, cut out the pages.

2. Choose the section
Place the first sheet face up on the cutting board. Disassemble one picture frame and move the mat around over the wallpaper until you like the part of the design that's framed.

3. Cut the pages
Use the pencil to trace around the outside edge of the mat. If pencil marks don't show on the wallpaper, cut small slits with the utility knife to mark each corner. Using the knife, and the ruler to keep a straight edge, cut out the wallpaper, staying just inside the pencil line or slits.

4. Reassemble the frame
Wipe any smudges off the glass with the dust cloth. Place the glass in the frame, then add the mat, the wallpaper, and the backing that came with the frame. Secure the edge clips or any other devices that hold the frame and art together. Repeat steps 2 through 4 for the other frames.

5. Hang the frames
To display the framed wallpaper in evenly spaced rows, use the hammer to tap a hanger or a nail into the wall at the middle of the top row. (If the walls are plaster, drill small holes for the hanger or nail before you tap it in so you don't crack the plaster.) Place one frame on the nail or the hanger. Hold another frame to one side and use the pencil to lightly mark where you want its top corners. Use the tape measure to determine the midpoint between the corners of the second frame and mark it with the pencil. Then adjust the midpoint up or down until the carpenter's level shows that the mark is level with the first picture hanger or nail. Attach the second hanger or nail there. Repeat the spacing between the first and second hangers or nails to establish the horizontal spacing for the other pictures. Determine the vertical spacing in a similar way, starting with the top middle picture. Hang your new artwork, arranging the frames as you like.

Style Note
Use white frames with pastel-colored wallpaper; use black or even gold frames for wallpaper that has brighter colors.

Alternate Method
If you can't get a free wallpaper sample book, check online for a company that sells wallpaper by the sheet.

7

Add style
with fabric

It's surprising what a difference fabric makes
to a room. Whether it's a pretty sink skirt in
the bathroom, an elegant piece of framed
fabric on the wall, or billowy curtains that
double as a canopy for your bed, fabric can
add dimension, color, and function to a
room. Sewing skills a little rusty? No problem. The step-by-step instructions in this
chapter will give you all the guidance you
need to staple, stitch, and glue to your
heart's content.

Ingenious Door ⩔

If you have an open closet, install a sliding curtain in a whimsical or elegant pattern that matches the bed linens or other elements in the room. It's pretty—and practical, too.

Window Style ⩓

A fabric window shade in the right colors or pattern can pull together a room's decor. If you can't find a ready-made shade that works, make your own by adding a fabric you love to an inexpensive roller shade.

Framed Flowers »

If you've ever fallen in love with a fabric pattern, now's the time to claim it for your home. No need to sew anything—just adhere it to a stretched canvas, with or without a frame (see page 144). Pig not included!

($) ($) ($)

Room divider

Do you have an office that doubles as a guest room, or a kids' room shared by dueling siblings? No need to put up a wall. Simply hang colorful curtains from a sliding track to create an instant room divider.

Materials

- curtains or draperies, at least ceiling height
- sliding curtain track, with carrier rollers and end caps
- iron-on hemming tape (if curtains need shortening)

Tools

- ladder or step stool
- tape measure
- hacksaw
- newspaper
- pencil or painter's masking tape
- 3-inch screws or toggle bolts
- drill with bits
- screwdriver
- needle or sewing machine, plus thread (if two or more curtains need to be sewn together)
- scissors
- iron, and ironing pad or ironing board (if curtains need shortening)
- drapery hooks (if curtains require them)

▶ Steps

1. Cut the track

Measure the distance between the walls where the curtain will be. Subtract the allowance needed for the end caps of the curtain track. The result is the total track length you'll need. With the hacksaw, cut the length or lengths of track you need. Sawing will create sharp metal shards, so work over sheets of newspaper.

2. Locate the joists

In the area where the curtain will hang, tap along the ceiling to locate the ceiling joists (the wooden framing above the ceiling). When you're under a joist, the hollow sound will change to a thud. Mark the locations of the joists with the pencil or painter's masking tape.

3. Install the track

Attach an end cap onto one end of the curtain track. Working from the other end, slip the carrier rollers or curtain hangers onto the track, then add the other end cap. Install the track on the ceiling as the manufacturer recommends. Some systems include mounting brackets, while others call for fastening the track directly to the ceiling. If the track passes under a joist or crosses below several of them, you probably just need to screw the brackets or track to the ceiling with screws long enough to reach into wood. Drill pilot holes first, using a bit slightly smaller than the screws. If you must fasten the parts to the ceiling where there is no framing above, use toggle bolts. Installing these is trickier and requires wider pilot holes; follow the directions on the package.

4. Tailor the curtain

If you need several curtain or drapery panels to span the space and want the fabric to move as one piece, sew the side edges of the curtains together. Then measure the curtain length. If the curtains are too long, trim the bottom edges until each curtain is the correct length plus enough for a hem. Then turn up the bottom edge and secure it with iron-on hemming tape. Let the fabric cool before you move the curtain to ensure that the tape is secure.

5. Hang the curtain

Attach the curtain(s) to the hangers, using drapery hooks as connectors if the curtains require them.

Style Note

Sliding curtain track comes in curved and flexible styles as well as straight sections. There are even double- and triple-track systems, which allow you to hang both sheer and opaque curtains so you can adjust the amount of privacy between the divided spaces.

First-Timer Tip

Select curtains that aren't too billowy, so they hang straight down and enclose the space—even if there's a breeze.

$ $ $

Billowy ceiling drape

If you love the look of a canopy bed, but don't have room for one, this ceiling drape is a pretty alternative. It's light and sweet, and creates a cozy feeling for anyone sleeping under it.

Materials

- two lined rod-pocket curtains, each 6 feet long and at least several inches wider than the bed
- two ⅝-inch-diameter dowels, as long as the curtains' width
- eight no. 6 eye screws
- sturdy twine

Tools

- tape measure
- pencil or chalk
- sewing pins
- sewing machine or needle
- thread
- vanishing fabric marker
- yardstick
- seam ripper
- power drill with bits
- screwdriver (optional)
- scissors

▶ Steps

1. Mark

With the tape measure and pencil or chalk, make two marks close to the top of the wall to indicate the curtain width, which should be slightly wider than the bed. Make a second set of two marks on the ceiling 3 feet out toward the foot of the bed.

2. Create the overlap

Place the curtains right side up, top end to top end. Pin them so the rod pockets overlap. With the sewing machine or needle, sew the curtains together there, leaving the rod pockets open so that you can still slip in a dowel.

3. Create the billow

From the overlapping rod pockets, measure 4 feet toward the hem of one curtain. Using the vanishing marker and the yardstick, draw a straight line across the curtain there. Draw a parallel line 1¼ inches closer toward the hem. Pin the lining of the curtain and its fabric together along the lines.

4. Create a new rod pocket

Sew along the lines that you pinned in step 3 to create a new rod pocket. Remove the pins. Then open up the ends of the new pocket with the seam ripper (see below).

5. Create the end flap

So that the right side of the fabric will show on both sides of the end flap, fold the bottom of the curtain (past the new rod pocket) toward the back and stitch down the edge next to the pocket.

6. Add the eye screws

With the drill, bore a pilot hole into the ends of both dowels, using a bit slightly smaller than the shaft of the eye screws. With the same bit, drill at each mark you made at the top of the wall in step 1. Aim the drill so the bit cuts into the molding or wood framing within the wall. Then, for a wood ceiling, as pictured here, drill pilot holes at the two marks on the ceiling that are farther out into the room. (If the ceiling is drywall or plaster, see Alternate Method below.) Twist eye screws into all these holes, using the screwdriver for extra leverage if you need it.

7. Hang the curtain

Slip the rods into the rod pockets. Arrange the curtains so that the lining will face the wall and ceiling. With the scissors, cut four pieces of twine 24 inches long. Tie the middle of each piece to one of the eye screws on each of the dowel ends. Then tie the twine to the corresponding eye screws above the bed and hang.

Create a new rod pocket

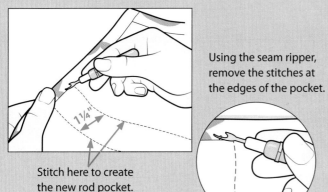

Using the seam ripper, remove the stitches at the edges of the pocket.

1¼"

Stitch here to create the new rod pocket.

First-Timer Tip

Drilling into a ceiling that contains asbestos would release harmful fibers, so do this project only if you know the ceiling is free of asbestos. (Popcorn ceilings, common in some areas of the country, often contain asbestos.)

Alternate Method

If you have a drywall or plaster ceiling, use two toggle bolts instead of eye screws to anchor the end of the fabric that's 4 feet from the wall. Instead of using standard bolts, use eye bolts with threads that fit the toggles.

$ $

DIY designer floor mat

Make your own floor mat by adapting a printed design you love, and add a personal touch and graphic punch to any room.

Materials

- decorative design on paper
- preprimed canvas floorcloth, 2 feet by 3 feet (available at crafts stores)
- latex enamel or artist's acrylic (background color), 1 quart
- latex enamel or artist's acrylic (design color), 8 ounces to 16 ounces
- matte clear acrylic, 1 quart

Tools

- art projector, available at crafts stores
- paint tray
- foam paint roller
- ruler
- masking tape, 1 inch or wider
- pencil, preferably 2B (softer than standard No. 2)
- artist's brush with flat, rounded tip, in a width suitable for your design
- scissors
- fabric glue or double-sided carpet tape

▶ Steps

1. Copy the design

Choose a design or decorative pattern from a book, or print one from the Web. Check the specifications on the art projector to determine the largest image you can work with. Then photocopy the pattern you selected to make it a size suitable for your floorcloth. Make a black-and-white copy; it will project best because the contrast is most vivid.

2. Paint the base coat

Pour the background color into the paint tray. With the roller, apply one coat, covering the entire front of the floorcloth. Let dry. Then, apply a second coat and let that dry.

3. Mark the hemming line

With the ruler, mark a 1-inch allowance on all the edges of the floorcloth to allow for hemming later. Only the image you paint within the hemming line will show later, but for ease of painting you can extend the design into the border.

4. Project and trace the pattern

Use the masking tape to hang the floorcloth on a wall in a room you can darken (so the projected image will be easier to see). Set the art projector (see photo at right) on a chair, bookcase, or other flat surface that's the right height to be even with the midpoint of the floorcloth as it is hanging. Place the photocopied pattern beneath the projector and move the projector and its support until the image appears on the  floorcloth in the desired size and within the hem allowance line. Use the pencil to trace the pattern onto the floorcloth. If the background color is dark, use chalk or a white pencil.

Style Note

Simple, high-contrast patterns work best because the projected image will show up well and the design will be easy to execute.

5. Paint the pattern

With the artist's brush, apply the second color between the lines to complete the design. If you are painting a light color onto a dark color and the first coat doesn't cover completely, you may need two coats. Let the paint dry between each layer.

6. Varnish

Pour the clear acrylic into the cleaned paint tray. With a clean roller, apply three thin coats of the clear acrylic. Let dry completely between coats.

7. Finish the edges

To create a hem with tidy mitered corners, use the pencil to mark the floorcloth edges 2 inches from each corner in both directions. With the ruler, draw a line connecting each pair of marks. Cut along each line with the scissors to remove a triangle of fabric from each corner. Fold under 1 inch on each edge of the floorcloth. Use fabric glue or double-sided carpet tape to secure the folds. If you use fabric glue, place books over the folds on the floorcloth to help set the glue as it dries; if you use tape, simply press firmly down on the floorcloth. Let the glue dry completely, and allow the clear acrylic finish to cure for at least a week before walking on your new mat.

First-Timer Tips

» Start painting along one edge of the floorcloth and rotate it as needed so you don't need to reach over fresh paint, risking a smear.

» If you use artist's acrylics, and the paint looks thick, thin it with a little water before use. Thick paint may crack when people walk on the floor mat.

($)

Framed fabric wall art

You want wall art but haven't found something you love at a price you can afford. The solution: Frame a gorgeous piece of fabric. It's instant art—and inexpensive enough that you can swap it out for a different pattern next year.

Materials
- light- or medium-weight fabric
- cardboard or poster board cut to fit in frame
- new or used picture frame, with or without glass

Tools
- iron, and ironing pad or ironing board
- sewing pins
- yardstick
- pencil
- scissors
- glue stick
- transparent or other type of tape
- heavy books to use as weights
- hammer
- picture hanger or nail

Steps

1. Iron the fabric
Set the iron to the appropriate temperature for the fabric. While the iron heats, place the fabric, right side down, on the ironing surface. Iron out any wrinkles.

2. Center the cardboard
Spread out the fabric, right side up, on a worktable. Position the cardboard on top so it rests over the part of the design you want to frame. Mark the corners of the cardboard by placing the pins in the fabric, catching just a few threads at each corner.

3. Mark and cut the fabric
Without moving the cardboard, place the yardstick alongside one edge of the cardboard. With the pencil, trace against the other side of the yardstick to create a border about an inch wide on the fabric. Repeat for the other edges. With the scissors, cut along the lines.

4. Wrap and glue the fabric
Flip the fabric so it's right side down. Center the cardboard on the back of the fabric, using the pins as guides. Apply a generous layer of glue in a 1-inch-wide band along all the edges of the cardboard. Starting in the middle of one side, fold over the excess fabric and press it in place. As you near each corner, fold the corner of the fabric straight back. Dab a little more glue and then fold the fabric on both sides of the corner back into a tidy miter. Tape down the miter.

5. Frame the fabric
Clean the glass on both sides. (Omit the glass if you want to emphasize the fabric's texture and aren't concerned about its longevity.) Place the frame upside down on a flat surface. Add the glass, then the framed fabric, then the frame's cardboard backing if it fits. Insert the fasteners that came with the frame. If you're using an old frame that doesn't have fasteners, use tiny brad nails and drive them sideways into the frame with the hammer. Then tap the picture hanger or nail into the wall and hang the framed fabric on it. (If the walls are plaster, drill a small hole for the hanger or nail before you tap it in so you don't crack the plaster.)

First-Timer Tip

Bring the frame to the fabric store and place it on the fabric before it's cut to length to make sure that the piece you choose includes the design elements you want to display.

Alternate Method

If you'd like to use heavyweight fabric or prefer not to have a frame, buy a stretched canvas from an art-supply store, cover it with the fabric, wrap the edges around the back, and staple them in place. Attach a picture hanger on the back to hang.

($) ($) ($)

Fabric pennants

As a simple decoration, flying pennants add quick color and a breezy cheerfulness to any room.

Materials

- two eye screws that the cord fits through (if needed—see step 1)
- two screw-in drywall anchors (if needed—see step 1)
- sash cord or other slender rope
- brightly colored fabric

Tools

- power drill with bits (if needed to install eye screws—see step 1)
- screwdriver (if needed to install eye screws—see step 1)
- scrap paper
- ruler
- pencil
- pinking shears or scissors
- transparent tape
- sewing pins
- sewing machine or needle
- thread
- scissors

Steps

1. Choose or create supports

If you have curtain rods, stairs with a balustrade, or other high features that you can wrap a cord around, you can attach the ends of your flag cord there. Otherwise, install eye screws. If you're fastening into wood, drill holes slightly smaller than the eye-screw shaft to install the eye screws. If you're fastening into drywall or plaster, use screw-in drywall anchors sized to the eye screw shaft.

2. Design the flags

Cut your flags out on scrap paper. A pleasing size is 12 inches long and 8 inches wide, but you can experiment with different sizes. To create even triangles, fold the paper in half lengthwise and draw a straight line that starts at the fold on one end and angles out to the edges at the other. Cut along the line, through both layers. Unfold the paper triangles and tape them to the cord to see how they look.

3. Make the pattern

When you have your dimensions, draw the shape you want on scrap paper. To allow for a hem where you can string the cord, add a band 1½ inches deep along the wide end of the triangle. Square the ends of the band, making it only as long as the wide end of the triangle.

4. Cut the fabric

Pin the pattern to one piece of fabric. With pinking shears, cut along its edges. To cut the maximum number of pennants from a single width of fabric, cut flags side by side, alternating the direction of the tip.

5. Sew

Leaving some cord free on one end, wrap the hem allowance of the first flag around the cord one full turn, so no raw edge is exposed. Pin through the flag to secure it to the cord. Stitch through the flag and the cord all along the hem. Sew on the remaining flags, leaving even spacing and some flag-free cord at the other end. Use the flag-free ends to tie up the cord.

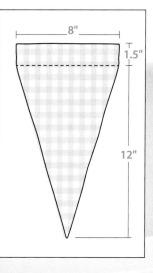

Style Note

Flags generally look best if they are longer than they are wide.

8"

1.5"

12"

Style Note

For an interesting mix of colors and patterns, visit a quilting store and buy different patterns in "fat quarters" (fabric pieces 18 inches by 22 inches) and "fat eights" (11 inches by 18 inches).

Maintenance Tip

If you don't have pinking shears, rub a little liquid seam sealer along any edges that were cut with standard scissors to keep flags from fraying over time.

($) ($)

Fabric-covered bulletin board

Do you paste sticky notes all over the house as reminders to yourself? Here's a more attractive option: a bulletin board. Use lightweight fiberboard and cover it in fun fabric.

Materials

- recycled-paper fiberboard, ½ inch thick (see step 1 for size)
- heavy-weave fabric, 4 inches in length and width beyond the bulletin board dimensions

Tools

- sewing pins
- yardstick
- pencil or chalk (depending on fabric color)
- handsaw or jigsaw
- scissors
- staple gun with ⅜-inch or 5⁄16-inch staples

▶ Steps

1. Mark the fiberboard

Decide on the bulletin board size you want; the one pictured here is 2 feet by 3 feet. Using the pencil and yardstick, mark the size on the fiberboard, using an end and one side as two of the final edges. Check that you drew square corners by measuring both diagonals across the shape; the distances should be equal.

2. Cut the fiberboard

Find a place to work where it's okay for some dust to fly. Using the saw, cut along your outline.

3. Cut the fabric

Drape the fabric, right side out, over the fiberboard. Adjust the fabric until the board is behind the part of the design you want to display. Mark the corners with sewing pins, catching only a few threads at each corner. Set the fiberboard aside. Spread out the fabric, right side down, on a flat work surface. Use the yardstick and the pencil (or chalk) to mark a 2-inch border beyond the pins. With the scissors, cut out the fabric along the lines.

4. Wrap the board

With the fabric still right side down on the work surface, center the fiberboard on the fabric. Starting on one edge a few inches from a corner, wrap the fabric around to the back of the fiber-board and staple it. (This strip of wrapped fabric should be about 1½ inches wide.) Continue in this manner, wrapping the fabric around that edge and stapling every 2 to 3 inches. Stop when you get a few inches from the next corner. Then repeat this process for the other three sides.

5. Complete the corners

To finish one corner, pull the corner of the fabric tight over the fiberboard, toward the center, and use a staple to secure the fabric to the back of the fiberboard. Create neat tucks with the remaining fabric in that corner and staple them down (see illustrations). Repeat for the other corners.

Style Note

Look for decorative pushpins that would be fun to use on your fabric: butterfly pins with floral fabric, fish pins on blue fabric, pink beaded pins on teal fabric.

First-Timer Tip

Heavyweight fabrics work best for this project because they stand up to being repeatedly pierced with thumbtacks or pushpins.

▶ Complete the corners

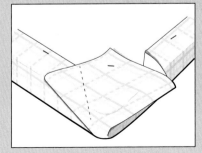

Pull the fabric tight at one corner and staple.

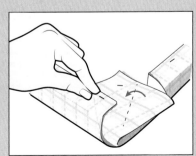

Create tucks with the remaining fabric.

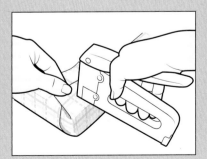

Staple the tucks.

($)

Faux Roman shades

Roman shades look as though they're drawn halfway up, but are actually sewn to cover just the top of the windows. Light and airy, they are perfect for rooms where you don't need a lot of privacy.

Materials
- decorator fabric, at least 4 inches wider than the window
- balsa wood, 1¼ inches by ¼ inch, cut ½ inch shorter than the shade width

Tools
- tape measure
- iron, and ironing pad or ironing board
- carpenter's square
- pencil
- yardstick
- scissors
- sewing pins
- thread
- sewing needle or sewing machine
- double-sided mounting tape, 1 inch wide
- hammer
- nails, 1 inch to 1½ inches long

▶ Steps

1. Measure

Measure the width you want for the shade, and write down the measurement. Then note how long you want the shade to hang and write that down. Add 4 inches to the width measurement so you can turn under the edges. Add 14 inches to the length measurement, allowing for one 3½-inch fold, two 2½-inch folds, a 2-inch double hem (for a total of 4 inches), and about 1½ inches for mounting.

2. Cut

Iron the fabric and place it wrong side up. Close to one end, use the carpenter's square and pencil to mark a straight line perpendicular to the uncut edge. Trace against the yardstick to extend the line across the fabric. From this baseline, measure and mark the lengths and widths you need. Then, with the scissors, cut out the shade fabric. (If the fabric isn't wide enough for the width you need, cut two lengths and sew them together, matching the pattern.)

3. Hem

Turn up 2 inches on the bottom of the fabric. Then fold that over again (in a double hem) to hide the cut edge. Iron, pin, and sew down the top fold to create a hem. Repeat on the sides, but make each fold only 1 inch deep.

Create the folds

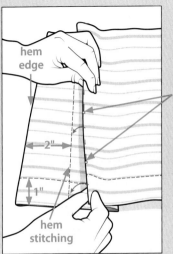

hem edge

2"

1"

hem stitching

Place a line of pins 3½" from the hem stitching. Pinch the line of pins into a fold and pull it down until it meets the hem stitching.

4. Create the folds

Place the fabric right side up, with the hem edge facing you. Place a line of pins 3½ inches up from the hem stitching. Pinch the line of pins into a fold and pull it down until it meets the hem stitching (see illustration). This will create a crease seen only on the back of the fabric. Iron that crease (from the front of the fabric). Remove the pins from the pin line and use them to pin along the crease, pinning through the front of the fabric. Place a few hand stitches every 3 inches along the crease (catching a few threads on the front of the fabric). Remove the pins as you go. Repeat two more times, but pin 2½ inches up from the previous line of hand stitches.

5. Assemble

Attach the mounting tape to the length of one side of the balsa wood. With the taped side of the wood facing up, align the top of the fabric with the top edge of the wood, and press the fabric down. Smooth the fabric as you press it against the tape. Flip the wood so the shade drapes over it, hiding the wood.

6. Attach

Hold the shade in position above the window. At one end of the balsa strip, maneuver the fabric out of the way and hammer a nail through the balsa and into the window frame or the wall (make sure you hit the wood framing). Repeat at the other side of the window. Then lift the shade and nail the rest of the balsa strip to the window frame or the wall.

First-Timer Tip

Striped fabric will create a nice tailored look if you keep all the stripes lined up; otherwise, the shades will look sloppy. Prints and solid-color fabrics are more forgiving than stripes, thus a safer choice for a first-timer.

Style Note

The instructions here are for a tailored look, as shown in the photograph. For a billowy look, don't iron the creases, and sew them down with only a few stitches at the side edges and in the middle.

($) ($)

Closet curtain

Plain sliding closet doors are certainly utilitarian, but most of them lack spunk. Why not switch them out for something more exciting, like colorful curtains?

Materials

- adjustable, tension-type curtain rod long enough to span the closet opening
- curtains (about the same height and 2 times the width of the door opening)
- iron-on hemming tape (if curtains need shortening)

Tools

- screwdriver (optional)
- ladder or step stool (if needed)
- ruler
- scissors
- drapery rings (with drapery hooks if curtain calls for them)
- iron, and ironing pad or ironing board (if curtains need shortening)

First-Timer Tip

Select curtains that are aren't too bulky so that, when the curtains are open, you can see most of what's inside the closet.

Steps

1. Remove the closet doors

With the screwdriver, remove the door guide on the floor, and then the tracks at the top.

2. Adjust the length

Measure the height of the opening, and subtract the allowance you need for the rod and drapery rings to find the length you need for the curtains. If they are too long, use the scissors to trim each curtain panel to the correct length plus enough for a hem. Then turn up the bottom edge of the curtains and secure it with the iron-on hemming tape. Let the fabric cool.

3. Install the rod

Adjust the rod's length and slip the drapery rings onto the rod. Then hold the rod in the closet opening and twist the rotating end until you get a snug fit. (Use a step stool if needed in order to get a better grip on the rod.)

4. Add the curtain

Hang the curtain panels, using the drapery hooks if needed.

($)

Sink skirt

Whether it's frilly or just fun, a fabric skirt is a great way to dress up a wall-mounted sink. Bonus: It also creates a practical place for bathroom storage by letting you hide toiletries and other bathroom essentials underneath.

Materials

- main skirt fabric (for yardage, see step 1)
- contrasting fabric, 1 yard
- corded piping trim
- hook-and-loop tape with sew-on and self-stick sides

Tools

- tape measure
- pencil and yardstick (to measure fabric)
- scissors
- iron, and ironing pad or ironing board
- thread
- sewing machine
- sewing pins

Steps

1. Cut the fabric

Measure the three exposed sides of the sink perimeter and multiply by 1½. That will be the horizontal dimension of the main fabric. Then measure the height you want for the total skirt length, and subtract 6 inches for the contrasting bands and their seams. Cut the main fabric to these dimensions. From the contrasting fabric, cut four strips 8 inches wide—three strips as long as the skirt perimeter and one strip an inch longer.

2. Create the bottom band

Sew the three same-length contrasting strips end to end, with right sides facing together and ½-inch-wide seams. Near each end of the resulting long strip, fold the fabric lengthwise with the right side in and sew across the band ½ inch from the short edges (see illustration below). Turn the fabric right side out. Fold the entire strip lengthwise and iron it flat.

3. Create the top band

Take the strip of contrasting fabric with the extra inch and iron it in half lengthwise, right side out, creating a crease. Open up the fabric and place it right side up. Sew the sew-on part of the hook-and-loop tape alongside the crease, to a single layer of fabric (see illustration on next page), stopping the tape ½ inch from each short edge. Fold the fabric so that the right side faces in. Sew across the fabric ½ inch from each short edge. Turn the fabric right side out and again fold it lengthwise. Iron it flat.

continued on next page

Create the bottom band

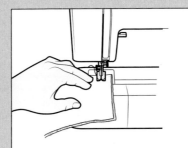

Sew ½ inch from the short edges, with right sides facing each other.

4. Hem the sides of the skirt

On each side edge of the main fabric, turn ½ inch to the back, then fold that over a second time, creating a double hem. Iron it flat, and sew the hem.

5. Create the gathers

Adjust the machine to its longest straight stitch. On the longer contrasting strip, sew lengthwise through both layers in two parallel lines, ½ inch and ⅜ inch from the cut edge. Pull on the bobbin threads to create gathers until the strip is short enough to match the bottom edge of the main fabric (see illustration). Then gather the top edge of the main fabric until it is as short as the top contrasting band.

6. Add the corded piping

On the right side of the fabric, sew the corded piping to the bottom edge of the main fabric and to the side of the top contrasting band that doesn't have hook-and-loop tape. In both cases, face the corded part of the piping away from the edge and stitch along the cord (see illustration). At the ends, turn the piping into the seam allowance.

7. Sew the bands to the skirt

At the bottom of the skirt, place the gathered edge band over the corded piping, overlapping all the raw edges. Pin in place, then flip over the layers so you can see the stitches from step 6. Sew over those, through all the layers, removing the pins as you go. Join the gathered top edge of the skirt to the top band in the same way.

8. Hang the skirt

Press the adhesive-backed hook-and-loop tape onto the sink perimeter and attach the skirt.

Style Note

For the skirt and ruffle, pair a pretty print with stripes that pick up the same colors (as pictured here), or mix polka dots and a plaid.

Create the top band

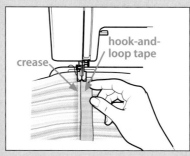

Starting ½ inch from the edge and leaving a ½-inch allowance, sew the hook-and-loop tape at one side of the crease.

Create the gathers

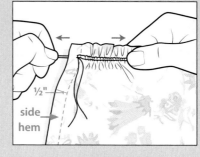

Pull on the bobbin threads to create gathers.

Add the corded piping

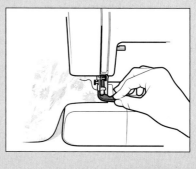

Face the corded side of the piping away from the raw edge of the fabric and stitch along the cord. Turn the piping into the seam allowance.

Alternate Method

For a no-sew alternative, start with a curtain that's gathered on the top. Adjust the length by affixing iron-on hemming tape to the bottom edge.

First-Timer Tip

Leave the skirt in place for at least 24 hours while the hook-and-loop adhesive reaches full strength. After that, you can remove the skirt for laundering, as needed.

($) ($) ($)

Fabric-covered footrest

Reinvent a solid-colored or worn footrest with colorful fabric.

Materials

(not including footrest)

- home decor fabric (for yardage, see step 1)

Tools

- tape measure
- yardstick
- carpenter's square
- pencil
- paper for patterns
- sewing pins
- scissors
- sewing machine
- thread

Style Note

Choose different patterns for each face of the footrest (as pictured here), or use one fabric that has a border design for all four sides. Or go with solid colors throughout but make each panel a different color.

▶ Steps

1. Measure the footrest and buy fabric

With the tape measure, determine the height, width, and depth of your footrest. Make a sketch and note the dimensions of the four side panels and one top panel. Add ½ inch for seam allowances at all edges except at the bottoms of the side panels; there, add 2 inches. Buy fabric.

2. Cut the fabric

Using the yardstick, square, and pencil, mark the fabric for the pieces you need. Cut out the fabric.

3. Sew the side panels together

Place two adjoining side panels with their mating edges lined up, right sides facing. Starting ½ inch from where you will eventually sew on the top piece, stitch the panels together ½ inch from the edges. Sew the other side seams in the same way, always leaving the top ½ inch unstitched (so you will be able to sew on the top without bunching up fabric at the corners). Iron the seams so the ½-inch seam allowances flare out on the wrong side of the fabric.

4. Pin the sides to the top panel

Arrange the fabric on a worktable so the top panel is face up and one side panel faces down. Line up the top edge of the side panel with one side edge of the top panel. Pin the two pieces together close to the edge, adding a pin at each end to keep the seam allowances folded back toward that side panel. Shift the fabric and pin another side. Repeat until the sides are all pinned to the top piece.

5. Sew the sides to the top panel

Position the pinned fabric on the sewing machine with the top panel facing up, and one side panel on top of it, facing down. Starting ½ inch from a corner, stitch the panels together ½ inch from the pinned edge (see illustration). Remove the pins as you go. Stop ½ inch from the next corner. With the needle lowered into the fabric, lift the presser foot and rotate the fabric a quarter-turn to round the corner. Lower the presser foot and continue to stitch along the top of the next side panel. Work your way around the top this way, always stopping ½ inch before the next corner. After completing the last side, pass over the final

Sew sides to the top panel

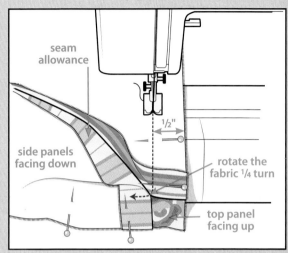

seam allowance

side panels facing down

½"

rotate the fabric ¼ turn

top panel facing up

Stitch the side panels to the top panel, rotating the fabric to round the corner.

corner and then stich over the first few inches of the stitches you made, to prevent unraveling.

6. Hem

Along the bottom edge, fold 1 inch toward the inside and then fold that over another inch. Iron the folds flat. Pin, then stitch the hem, removing pins as you go. Turn the fabric right side out and slip it over the footrest.

First-Timer Tips

» If you use striped fabric, orient the stripes in opposite directions on neighboring panels (as pictured here). This creates a sharp look and you will avoid the possibility of the lines not matching up on the neighboring panels.

» If you can, buy preshrunk fabric for easy laundering. Otherwise, buy a little extra fabric to allow for shrinkage and wash and dry the material before you cut.

Credits

Photography

ACP/Richard Birch/trunkarchive.com: 70 top right; ACP/James Geer/trunk archive.com: 10; ACP/Maree Homer/trunkarchive.com: 14 left, 53, 71, 88, 133; ACP/Tim James/trunkarchive.com: 22 top left; ACP/Louise Lister/trunkarchive.com: 137; ACP/Prue Ruscoe/trunkarchive.com: 39, 70 bottom left, 156; ACP/Rhiannon Slatter/trunkarchive.com: 145; ACP/Chris Warnes/trunkarchive.com: 2 right, 68–69, 77, 79, 80; Serge Anton/Living Inside: 101; Lincoln Barbour: 47 (Design: Jesse Moyer); Rob D. Brodman: 90–91 (Project: Birte Walter; styling: Miranda Jones), 94 both, 96 (Project: Birte Walter; styling: Miranda Jones), 97 (Project: Birte Walter; styling: Miranda Jones), 98 inset, 98 main (Project: Birte Walter; styling: Miranda Jones), 100 (Project: Birte Walter; styling: Miranda Jones), 105 inset, 105 main (Project: Birte Walter; styling: Miranda Jones), back cover top (Project: Birte Walter; styling: Miranda Jones); Robbie Capponetto: 59; James Carrier: 73 inset, 142 main (Patterns courtesy of Kawade Shobo Shinsha Publishers and Takashi Katano, printed in *Designer's Guide to Japanese Patterns* series, by Jeanne Allen), 143; Jeffery Cross: 1, 24, 27 both, 32, 36, 55 all (Styling: Miranda Jones), 103 inset (Project: Aaron Jones); GAP Interiors/Johnny Bouchier: 12; GAP Interiors/Bieke Claessens: 75; GAP Interiors/Douglas Gibb: 108 bottom left; GAP Interiors/Bill Kingston: 14 right; William Geddes: 18–19 (Stylist: Marcus Hay), 37 (Stylist: Marcus Hay); Tria Giovan: 42 bottom left, 60; Daniel Hennessy: 45; Bjarni B. Jacobsen & Flora Dania/Pure Public/Living Inside: 106–107, 113, 114; Tim James/Taverne Agency: 117; David Jordan/IPC+ Syndication: 136 top right; Chuck Kuhn: 28; Dave Lauridsen: 38; Andrew Lehmann: 134–135, 148; James Merrell/IPC+ Syndication: 85; Matthew Millman: 73 main (Design: Jay Jeffers, Jeffers Design Group); Laura Moss: 9 top left, 34 (Interior design: Jamie Herzlinger), 58 (Architect and design: Schappacherwhite LTD); Ngoc Minh Ngo/Taverne Agency: 92 bottom left; Photoshot/Red Cover/David George: 22 bottom left; Photoshot/Red Cover/Robin Matthews: 22 top right; Photoshot/Red Cover/Anastassios Mentis: 22 bottom right; Photoshot/Red Cover/Ed Reeve: 152; Lisa Romerein: 9 bottom left; Andrea Gómez Romero: 150 (Design: Kishani Perera); Eric Roth: 42 top right, 57 (Design: Susan Sargent Designs), 65 (Design: Susan Sargent Designs), 153 (Design: Susan Sargent Designs), 155 (Design: Susan Sargent Designs); Alexandra Rowley: 123, 125; Annie Schlechter: 2 left, 6–7, 9 bottom right, 11, 29 (Design: Sasha Adler), 43; Rachael Smith/Gap Interiors: 81; Thomas J. Story: 2 center, 9 top center (Prop styling: Sheherazade Arasnia), 9 top right, 13, 17, 25, 33, 40–41, 49 (Styling: Molly Hurd), 51, 83 both, 87 (Project and styling: Miranda Jones), 103 main (Project: Aaron Jones), 108 top right, 109, 111 (Styling: Molly Hurd), 118 (Styling: Miranda Jones; wallpaper by Ferm Living), 120 (Styling: Miranda Jones; wallpaper by Ferm Living), back cover bottom; Tim Street-Porter: 62 (Design: Michael K. Bell Interior Design), 67 (Design: Joseph Giovannini), 140 (Design: Heather Chadduck); Superstock: 126; Lucinda Symons/Country Homes & Interiors/IPC+ Syndication: 92 top right; E. Spencer Toy: 20, 142 inset; Chris Tubbs/Gap Interiors: 147; Amanda Turner/GAP Photos/Getty Images: 136 bottom left; Mikkel Vang/Taverne Agency: 9 bottom center; Dominique Vorillon: 16, 21, 138 (Architect/design: Barbara Bestor); Bjorn Wallander: Front cover (Art direction: Philippine Scali; styling: Ethel Brennan; stylist assistants: Jesse Long and Jennifer Hale; props: dresser from Ikea, bowl by Alex Marshall; artwork: Le typograph; pillow: Hable Construction); 4–5 (Art direction: Philippine Scali; styling: Ethel Brennan; stylist assistants: Jesse Long and Jennifer Hale; artwork: Le typograph), 93 (Art direction: Philippine Scali; styling: Ethel Brennan; stylist assistants: Jesse Long and Jennifer Hale; props: dresser from Ikea, bowl by Alex Marshall, artwork from Le typograph, pillow from Hable Construction), 131 and back cover (Styling: Ethel Brennan; decal: Blik Design); Polly Wreford/navalis images.com: 15, 31, 129

Illustration

Haisam Hussein: 89, 95, 112, 115, 124, 141, 147, 149, 151, 154, 157
Margaret Sloan: 87

Special Thanks

Jess Chamberlain, Erika Ehmsen, Mark Hawkins, Miranda Jones, Charla Lawhon, Megan Lee, Laura Martin, Haley Minick, Marie Pence, Alan Phinney, Lorraine Reno, Margaret Sloan, Katie Tamony, Angela Tolosa

Index